# IMAGES OF WAR
# HITLER'S PANZERS

## RARE PHOTOGRAPHS FROM WARTIME ARCHIVES

### IAN BAXTER

Pen & Sword
**MILITARY**

First published in Great Britain in 2006 by
**P E N  &  S W O R D  M I L I T A R Y**
an imprint of
Pen & Sword Books Ltd,
47 Church Street, Barnsley,
South Yorkshire.
S70 2AS

ISBN 1-84415-490-4

A CIP catalogue record for this book is available
from the British Library

Printed and bound in Great Britain by CPI UK


*Pen & Sword Books Ltd incorporates the imprints of*
Pen & Sword Aviation, Pen & Sword Maritime,
Pen & Sword Military, Pen & Sword Select, Pen & Sword Military Classics,
Leo Cooper, Wharncliffe Local History

*For a complete list of Pen & Sword titles please contact:*
**PEN & SWORD BOOKS LIMITED**
47 Church Street, Barnsley, South Yorkshire, S70 2AS, England.
E-mail: enquiries@pen-and-sword.co.uk
Website: www.pen-and-sword.co.uk

# Contents

# Acknowledgements

It is with the greatest pleasure that I use this opportunity on concluding this book to thank those who helped make this volume possible. My expression of gratitude first goes to my friend and photographic collector Rolf Halfen. He has been an unfailing source, supplying me with the bulk of the Panzer collection from numerous private albums that have been shut away for many years. Rolf has searched and contacted numerous collectors across Germany. Some of them would not part with their prized Panzer photographs, which made finding the later variant models so much harder. Armoured vehicles like the Hummel, Hetzer 38(t), Wespe, Nashorn and the even rarer models like the Jagdpanther and Jagdtiger, were difficult to say the least to find unpublished. I had numerous researchers trying to locate these elusive vehicles, but it was Rolf once again that managed to find them in private photo collections in Germany.

Further a field in Poland I am also extremely grateful to Marcin Zboiska, my Eastern Front photographic specialist, who supplied me with a number of rare photographs that he obtained from a private photographic collector in the Ukraine. The images he found show a host of interesting various models including late variant Panzerkampfwagen.IV`s, Panthers, and Tigers. I was even handed a unique batch of images showing armoured regiments of the Bulgarian Army, that show new Panzers being delivered from Germany to Bulgaria on direct orders from Hitler. Although the Bulgarian Panzers did not see combat on the Eastern Front against the Red Army, it is still a fascinating glimpse of how the vehicles were utilised for a specific anti-partisan role in the Balkans.

All other images in this book are credited to the HITM Archive.
hitm.archive@tiscali.co.uk

# Foreword

Although it was the British that invented tank warfare, it was the Germans that mastered it. This book describes how the Panzer evolved and how new fighting vehicles gained sufficient mobility and firepower to spearhead the Nazi Blitzkrieg through Europe. From the early victorious campaigns in 1939 and 1940, to the last ditch defence in Germany in 1945, each chapter features rare and unseen Panzer photographs and analyses these vehicles that dominated Europe, North Africa and the vast wastelands of the Soviet Union.

The sole purpose of this book is to share unpublished photographs with the military historian and enthusiast alike that both have a fascination with German armoured warfare of World War Two. The majority of the photographs collected are from private collections and are a simple volume of amateur snap-shots taken by ordinary German soldiers or Panzer crews. The entire collection has been reproduced in high digital format resolution from the original image. The reader may find that some of the photographs are slightly blurred, discoloured, scratched, soiled with various dust particles or dirt. But what makes this unpublished collection unique is that all the images have been untouched. There has been no digital enhancement to the image or any cropping. What the reader sees is what the photographer saw through his lens the moment the cameras shutter captured a part of history. For this reason alone the photographs in this book are an invaluable source that illustrates the importance of the development, the success and the final destruction of Hitler`s once vaunted armoured force.

In each chapter the photographs primarily illustrate the different variant model Panzers that were produced and saw action on the battlefield. Although some of the photographs are posed snap-shots of soldiers or tank crews with their armoured vehicles, the images still vividly portray a realism, which many press photographs failed to achieve. Most of the Panzers in this volume are photographed advancing to the front, paused during a brief break in the fighting, or simply under repair in one of the many workshops. There contains limited action images. Real action photographs were relatively a rare occurrence and seldom did a photographer risk his life armed with just a camera. The majority of the action photographs in circulation today were taken by press agencies, many of which can clearly be seen as staged propaganda pieces of photographic memorabilia. Although they provided the reader with a detailed testament to how these Panzers were used, appeared, and fought in combat, their glossy unblemished appearance seemed to take away the true grit of war from an actual soldiers point-of-view. What makes this book different is that the photographs portray the Panzer war from a soldier's perspective. The amateur photography captivates every aspect of the Panzer and the dedicated men who fought with them with such deadly effect. This book is undoubtedly a vivid and fully illustrated account of the development and deployment of Hitler's Panzer's seen through the lens of the soldiers that marched and fought with them.

A Pz.Kpfw.II Autumn of 1941 on the Eastern Front. This was one of the most popular vehicles seen during the early years of the war. However, by the time it entered Russia in the summer of 1941 it soon became apparent that it was no match against some of the heaviest Soviet armour.

# Chapter One

# Development & Training

Even during the 1920's it was apparent that, for the modern army, the consequences of entering soldiers onto a battle field without proper armoured support, would be suicidal. This of course is one reason Germany were not allowed a tank force under the Versailles Treaty. However, once Adolf Hitler came into power the conditions of the treaty were slowly usurped for his own military purposes of secret expansion. What followed in the early 1930's was a period of covert experimentation which led to the development of the tank. In total secrecy the *Kleintraktor*, the forerunner of the *Panzerkampfwagen*.I, was moved to the tank proving grounds at Kama where its design and all the technical aspects of the machine was put through a series of tests. At the same time the crews and officers received practical training in the use of tanks in battle. Although the training went well there was only a very limited number of machines available, and it was clearly insufficient as a tank force.

However, by January 1934 the first 150 *Kleintraktor* chassis for driver training commenced. From this point the rapid expansion of the tank forces could proceed. As training continued throughout 1934 tank designers had been working on a new armoured vehicle, which was a modified version of the *Kleintraktor*. It was known at the time as the *MG Panzerwagen,* but technically it was called the *Panzerkampfwagen*.I. It was the first vehicle to be designed and produced in any significant numbers. At this point it was the first serious tank the Germans had ever built, and the variants that would be produced from this first model were to bring much success to the *Wehrmacht* during the Second World War. Delivery of 318 *Panzerkampfwagen.I* was made in August 1935, along with 15 of the *Zugführerwagen,* which was later to be known as the *Panzerkampfwagen*.III.

Excises with the new tanks began almost immediately with special attention being made to train its forces in close co-operation between the airforces and the Panzers on the ground. It was soon realised that the Panzers had three main tasks: supporting infantry, operating units with other mobile weapons and, finally, combating tanks. Even during this early period of training it was decided that the light tanks, such as the new *Panzerkampfwagen*.I, would be used in a scouting role and that an infantry support tank would be developed which was ultimately to come in the form as the *Panzerkampfwagen.IV.* Although it was well known that the *Panzerkampfwagen.I* was inadequate for most purposes on the battlefield it made an excellent training tank for the Panzer crews of the future.

In fact, in 1936 when Germany gave its support to the Nationalist forces during the Spanish Civil war, Hitler immediately sent a Panzer unit consisting mainly of *Panzerkampfwagen.I*'s to support the Nationalists drive on Madrid. To Hitler the use of a tank unit was of great importance to the development and training of his Panzers, in spite of the limitations of the *Panzerkampfwagen.I*. Much has been written on the poor performance of this small Panzer during the Spanish Civil war, but the use of the Panzer unit was more about the strategy and importance in the employment in mobile tank operations than its firepower, for Hitler had already switched resources to bigger and more powerful models.

By the end of 1936 the *Panzerkampfwagen.II* left the production line for service and rose steadily the following year. During 1937 the *Panzerkampfwagen.III* made its debut followed by the *Panzerkampfwagen.IV* in January 1938. With these new tanks enrolled in the service of the Reich it boosted the strength of the under-equipped and still expanding *Panzertruppe*. Heinz Guderian the newly promoted General de *Panzertruppen* had helped transform this outdated and depleted Panzer force into a superb fighting machine. He had not only argued in favour of the bold employment of tanks en masse on the battlefield, but he had formulated the concept of the tank-led Blitzkrieg. Even the 2,700 tanks, which were ready for action by the summer of 1939, were regarded more than enough to crush Germany's first victim of the Second World War, Poland. Although this Panzer strength was well below what Guderian had initially said was necessary if victory was assured, the *Panzertruppen* had something no one else had acquired in so full a measure – specially selected and very well trained Panzer crews. These elite band-of-brothers in their dramatic black Panzer uniforms owed much to their training as they did to their superior vehicles which they fought with such deadly effect on the battlefield. It is perhaps testimony to these courageous and fiercely dedicated men of the *Panzertruppen* that led them to survive the vicious battles that raged for almost six years.

The forerunner of the mighty Panzers. Because the Treaty of Versailles had strictly forbidden the Germans to develop any type of armoured force, the *Wehrmacht* were compelled to build wood and cardboard frames placed over the chassis of converted vehicles.

A photograph showing the type of materials used to construct one of the many converted wood and cardboard training vehicles. The covert use of these vehicles was the beginning of the experimentation that lead to the development of the first Panzer force.

Workshop engineers can be seen making adjustments to one of the fist training Panzers, the *Panzerkampfwagen.I A*, also known as the LaS. This vehicle is being prepared for training purposes in 1934. It was nicknamed the 'Krupp-Sport' by the soldiers, and was the forerunner of the *Panzerkampfwagen.I Ausf.A*.

Out on the training ground in 1934 this LaS vehicle is being put through a series of gruelling tests prior to its first training exercise with a crew. The driving school vehicles usually had no turret and only one rail around the open driver's compartment.

Recruits put the LaS through its paces during training exercises in 1934. The crew are demonstrating the versatility of the vehicle by using rough terrain. The open compartment with no turret gave the driver all round visual and a better understanding of the tanks mobility.

A posed camera shot showing the LaS during a training exercise. Although during training there was sometimes three or even four recruits onboard the vehicle at any one time, the LaS was actually designed for a two-man crew, one serving as the driver and the other as the commander, radioman and machine gunner.

After carefully hoisting and securing in place the air-cooled Krupp M 305 boxer engine, mechanics ease the 13mm engine cover plate over the rear of the *Panzerkampfwagen*.I Ausf.A. The engine had four horizontally opposed cylinders, which produced 60 HP at 2500 rpm. But the power-to-weight ratio of the engine meant that the tank was extremely underpowered.

An LaS during a training exercise. The vehicle had a top speed of 37 kph, and off-road rang of 145 kilometres. It could climb a slope of 58%, surmount vertical barriers to a height of 36 cm, span ditches 1.40 meters wider and ford water up to a depth of 57cm.

A *Panzerkampfwagen*.I Ausf.B in a field in 1937. The Ausf.B variant only proved to be slightly better than the Ausf.A model. The vehicles length was slightly increased to 4.42 meters, the height to 1.96 meters, while the width remained the same. Due to the increased weight the new engine was less efficient than the Ausf.A boxer engine, so the tanks range was decreased to only 130 kilometres.

New recruits are dressed in white training uniforms in 1937, prior to manoeuvres with their *Panzerkampfwagen*.I. Ausf.B vehicles. Throughout the late thirties rigorous drills and various battlefield tactics were instilled in the young recruits. The *Panzerkampfwagen*.I was well suited for training purposes and remained so throughout the war.

In the years before the war many civilians greeted the Panzer enthusiastically. Here in this photograph young German children are shown round a *Panzerkampfwagen.I*. Note that the vehicles weapons have been removed, which may indicate that the tank is more than likely on manoeuvres. Both the tank men are wearing the new distinctive black Panzer uniform. The tank man on the left is wearing the Panzer *Feldmütze* for officers, indicating he is the commander.

*A Pz.Kpfw.I during operations in France in 1940. Although undergunned, underpowered and sometimes prone to be mechanically unreliable, this armoured vehicle fought relatively well in spite of being up against sometimes much heavier and superior vehicles.*

A Pz.Kpfw.I moves along a road probably in the summer of 1940. During pre-war training and whilst operating in Poland, France and Russia, the Pz.Kpfw.I was normally finished in the early Panzer two-tone colour scheme of dark grey, over sprayed with dark brown.

The crew of a *Panzerkampfwagen*.I Ausf.B show the versatility of the tank by spanning ditches and various other obstacles. This type of training method was an important factor, as the tank would be employed on the battlefield in highly mobile operations crossing all types of various terrains in order to exploit breakthroughs on the battlefield.

A posed photograph showing a *Panzerkampfwagen.*I Ausf.A bulldozing through a brick wall. The vehicles 13mm armoured plating was more than capable of sustaining such an impact. However, its thin armour would soon prove a disappointment during the Spanish Civil War and later the war against Poland and France.

*Panzerkampfwagen.*I's on a popular military exercise in 1938. The most important part of Panzer training, apart from technical training on how to operate the vehicle itself, was on how to use the tank as an efficient weapon of war. Here in this photograph the tanks have broken cover and are moving in wide open-terrain in a 'V' formation. A flare has been ignited to signal the attack.

A photograph showing three *Panzerkampfwagen*.II's in a workshop. Until the *Panzerkampfwagen*.III and *Panzerkampfwagen*.IV entered service, German factories ordered the mass production of the *Panzerkampfwagen*.II. This light Panzer weighing 8.8 tons was powered by a 140 bhp Maybach HL62 TRM engine. Between 1937 and 1939 four variants were built, the Ausf.B, Ausf.C, Ausf.D and Ausf.E.

A *Panzerkampfwagen*.II undergoing a series of trials across some sandy terrain. The light Panzer is missing its 2cm KwK 30 L/55 gun. Many of the vehicles being put through their paces were unarmed, only later receiving their armament. In spite of extensive development of the *Panzerkampfwagen*.II, the vehicle was under-gunned and suffered from minimal protection.

A group of *Panzerkampfwagen*.II's during a training exercise in southern Germany. The vehicles are being filmed by a cameraman and probably used for propaganda purposes. After the outbreak of the war, the Panzer featured regularly in both newspapers and newsreels, reporting on Germany's initial great successes during the Blitzkrieg period.

# Chapter Two

# Panzerkampfwagen.I

In 1931 the need for the development of a light training Panzer to train the future personnel of the Panzer divisions finally went to the drawing table. Under the strictest of secrecy for the next three years a number of light Panzer prototypes were submitted, modified and tested. In 1933 Krupp designed a prototype called the LKA.I. This vehicle was partially based on the British Carden Loyd Mk.IV tankette chassis, two of which were secretly purchased from Russia. In the summer of 1933 Krupp's design was once again modified. This time it was decided to mount Krupp's chassis with a Daimler-Benz's superstructure and turret. In early February 1934 further tests were performed and improved. The Panzer they had finally developed was known as the *MG Panzerwagen Versuchkraftfahrzeug* 617. When the vehicle entered production it was renamed the *Panzerkampfwagen.I* or Pz.Kpfw.I Ausf.A. In April 1934, 15 brand new Ausf.A variants were presented to Heinz Guderian to his *Führer*. The Pz.Kpfw.I Ausf.A and Ausf.B, which were built in 1935, were very similar models, but both had different suspensions and engines. The Pz.Kpfw.I Ausf.A was experimentally mounted with a Krupp M601 diesel engine, but it was soon found to be underpowered and subsequently rejected.

The Pz.Kpfw.I Ausf.A, also called 'Krupp-Sport' by the soldiers, was a very noisy vehicle on account of its opposed air-cooled engine. The Ausf.B, however, was slightly quieter with a water-cooled engine. In spite of the noise the two-man crew adapted well in the tanks small cramped compartment. One crewmember served as driver, whilst the other fulfilling all other tasks in the vehicle as a commander, machine-gunner and radioman. The armament consisted of two machine guns side by side in the turret, with an effective shot range no more than 300 meters. Inside the vehicle it carried some 3,125 rounds of ammunition, which was quite impressive at that time.

The Pz.Kpfw.I first saw action during the Spanish Civil War in 1936, where both the tank and tactic of Blitzkrieg were finally put to the test. Some 100 Ausf.A, Ausf.B and *Kleiner* Panzer *Befehlswagen.I* tanks saw service with the Condor Legion under the command of Major Ritter von Thomas's Panzer *Abteilung* 88, also know as *Abteilung Drohne*. During the civil war the Pz.Kpfw.I practised concentrated attacks and breakthrough techniques. However, within a few months it was soon obvious that the light tank did not have any combat potential. It had suffered from an underpowered engine, uncompetitive armament and too-thin armour plate.

With its poor performance the vehicle was consequently developed into making it a fast reconnaissance and light infantry tank. What followed was the introduction of the Ausf.C, Ausf.D and Ausf.F variants. These vehicles were completely re-designs sharing only a limited number of components with the Ausf.A and Ausf.B. The Ausf.C was manufactured from late 1942 to early 1943. Some 40 of these variants were deployed on the battlefield and saw action in Russia, North Africa and Italy. The Ausf.D was an improved version of the Ausf.C and was up-armoured, but they were only produced in limited numbers. The Pz.Kpfw.I Ausf.F was another new model that entered service between 1942 and 1943, with only 30 being produced. The Ausf.F saw action on the Eastern Front with the 2.Panzer-Division. A few Ausf.C were deployed in Normandy in 1944, where they were all destroyed.

During the Polish campaign in September 1939, the Pz.Kpfw.I was the main Panzer of the German Army with some 1,445 in service. By the end of the Polish campaign a total of 89 of them had been knocked out of action. The following year when Hitler unleashed his forces against the Low Countries and France there were 640 Pz.Kpfw.I's deployed for front line combat, half the amount used against Poland. Eleven months later in June 1941, when the *Wehrmacht* attacked Russia some 410 Pz.Kpfw.I's were distributed between the 24 Panzer and 12 motorised divisions. Although many of the Pz.Kpfw.I's had been withdrawn from service which had formed the majority of front-line tank strength in the Polish and French campaigns, they were still used to help provide the main armoured punch during the first few months of Barbarossa. During the French campaign it became apparent in tank versus tank combat of the deficiency of the Pz.Kpfw.I. In Russia however, fortunately for the *Wehrmacht,* the light Panzers had succeeded destroying the bulk of enemy armour for most of the Russian tanks were poor quality. But steps had already been taken to remedy these deficiencies and new Russian vehicles like the T-34 and KV-1 were far in advance of anything the *Wehrmacht* could field. Consequently huge losses were inflicted on the Pz.Kpfw.I, and those that remained in service were withdrawn and relegated to training Panzer crews or handed over to the Police and anti-partisan units.

During the North African campaign, where the Pz.Kpfw.I saw limited service, a small number of them were converted into *Flammenwerfer auf Panzerkampfwagen.I Ausf.A.* The vehicle was armed with a light portable *Flammenwerfer* (Flamethrower model) 40 and machine gun, in place of the right hand machine gun. Although this converted light tank was still a rare sight in the Western desert of North Africa, it was not the first time that the Pz.Kpfw.I had been converted. In fact, between 1939 and 1940 some 100 Ausf.A and B variants were converted into various self-propelled gun carrying anti-tank vehicles, like the *Panzerjäger*.I, and *Sturmpanzer*.I *Bison*. They were also converted and used as ammunition carriers, recovery and light bridging vehicles, explosive charge layer, mine clearing, and an armoured ambulance.

   Although the Pz.Kpfw.I had not truly been a combat tank, Panzer designers and manufacturers had been given valuable experience in design and producing the next generation of new Panzers that were soon to emerge on the battlefield. As for the Panzers crews, they continued to train with them throughout the war in order to attain the knowledge and experience of Panzer warfare before stepping onboard larger and more potent vehicles.

A group of Pz.Kpfw.I's at a training camp in 1938. By the time war broke out in Poland the following year these vehicles would have their distinctive white painted crosses on the side of the turret. Thankfully for the *Panzerwaffe* these Panzers faced very little opposition in Poland.

A line of
Pz.Kpfw.I's Aus
in late 1938. T
twin MG 13
machine guns
were removed
from all comb
vehicles before
they were par
It was also
standard pract
that all radio
equipment wa
be removed fr
the armoured
vehicles.

Workshop engineers pose for the camera with a Pz.Kpfw.I Ausf.A. These vehicles are being prepared to march. The first test for the Pz.Kpfw.I was the Spanish Civil War, where they were used by German volunteers of the 'Legion Condor'. The second test – though not with live ammunition – was the march into the Sudetenland in late 1938.

A Pz.Kpfw.I Ausf.A has halted on a road after experiencing some problems with the vehicles drive wheel. A civilian has come to the aid of the crewmen with water. The tracks of the Ausf.A had a ground pressure of only 780 g/sq.cm and gave the vehicle sufficient off road capability. The ground pressure was extremely good, but because the engine was so underpowered it was prone to mechanical problems.

The crew of a Pz.Kpfw.I Ausf.A pose for the camera during a brief break in a training exercise. The main armament has been removed and placed in storage whilst the vehicle was put through its paces. The man in the turret is in fact the trainer, whilst the other two men are the crewmembers dressed in the familiar denim training tunics.

During the occupation of the Sudetenland in October 1938. A group of tank men from an unknown Panzer regiment converse among themselves around a stationary Pz.Kpfw.I. Ausf.A. Not a single shot was fired in anger when the Wehrmacht rolled into the Sudetenland. Note that the vehicle MG 13 machine guns still have the protected canvas covering over the barrels.

The Pz.Kpfw.I. Ausf.A could cross flat dry terrain relatively easily and could be steered without too much trouble. The driver controlled the direction by means of steering levers, each of which had two handgrips, one for normal steering and the other with a thumb-plunger to act as a parking brake.

A Panzer unit during a pause in a drill. The crewman of these Pz.Kpfw.I. Ausf.A's are wearing the standard black Panzer uniform, a jacket with rose coloured shoulder boards, collar patches and jacket trim. The black berets were worn over a hard rubber liner to protect the head from injury in the Panzer.

Two Pz.Kpfw.I. Ausf.A's advance along a dirt road. During the Polish Campaign it was soon realized that this light tank could not withstand antitank fire. Only small calibre weapons fire and shell fragments would bounce off the 13mm armoured plating. Mines and hits from 2cm shells could easily knock them out of action.

An interesting photograph showing an unidentified Panzer regiment halted inside a town following the bloodless conquest of Bohemia and Moravia in March 1939. Note the camouflage scheme of this Pz.Kpfw.I. Ausf.A. It consisted of overall dark gray with dark green patches over the whole vehicle. Later in the France and Russia they were mainly finished in overall grey.

A crewmember of a Pz.Kpfw.I. Ausf.A poses in front of his vehicle prior to an exercise in early 1939. At the garrison training camps, there were large firing ranges and vast open areas of countryside where these vehicles could be used.

A trainer poses from the turret of a Pz.Kpfw.I Ausf.A. The new Panzer recruit adapted very well to this light tank where the crew used it extensively. Over a period of weeks the men learnt how to deploy the Panzer quickly and effectively and were taught the untried tactics of Blitzkrieg.

Trainers and their recruits prior to a gruelling exercise on the Lüneburg Heath. In order to prepare the men for battle stations the trainer would blow his whistle to signal the Panzer men to board their vehicles. Getting quickly inside the light tank was practiced frequently by the crews.

One of the most common problems of the Pz.Kpfw.I was its unreliability, especially in the Ausf.A model. Because the Krupp M 305 boxer engine was so underpowered it put unnecessary strain on the vehicles mechanics and consequently over heated the air-cooled system. In this photograph a Pz.Kpfw.I is being towed very slowly by a *Panzerwagen* LaS training vehicle after it had developed mechanical problems.

A posed photograph showing a father and his young child dressed in a Panzer uniform inside the turret of a Pz.Kpfw.I. Ausf.A. Prior to the war not all tanks had been equipped with radio equipment, and most of the communication was done with variously coloured signal flags in combat training.

On manoeuvres a Pz.Kpfw.I.Ausf.A has halted on a dirt road during an exercise in Germany. It is difficult to ascertain whether the soldier is a training instructor or not, but the uniform he is wearing clearly indicates that he is neither a new recruit nor a Panzer crewman. On a number of occasions, however, infantry did train alongside the Panzers in order to learn various tactics of close supporting roles with armour. This kind of training continued throughout the war.

A group of new Panzer recruits with a trainer pose for the camera with an armed Pz.Kpfw.I.Ausf.A during a training exercise in 1939. Note all the men are wearing their Panzer uniforms and beret. It was in 1934 that the first Panzer jacket and beret was introduced and was replaced two years later by the second issue Panzer jacket. The beret, however, remained in service with the Panzer crews until it was phased out in January 1941.

On 1 September 1939, 52 divisions and a formidable force of tanks attacked Poland. Some 1,445 Pz.Kpfw.I's were distributed among the new Panzer divisions and quickly drove into the heart of Poland. Here in this photograph a Pz.Kpfw.I is on exercise prior to the Polisu campaign. Luckily for the Pz.Kpfw.I barbed wire and a few anti-tank ditches were the only form of real defence.

A Pz.Kpfw.I.Ausf.A more than likely on a training exercise in 1940. This photograph was more than likely taken prior to the campaign in France in May 1940. The tank still retains its original old dark grey colour, however, by this period of the war the old white crosses originally used on the tanks during the Polish campaign have been removed and replaced with new Balkenkreuz.

A well camouflaged Pz.Kpfw.I.Ausf.B during the invasion of France in May 1940. Lots of foliage has been applied to the bulk of the vehicle, not only to conceal it among the undergrowth, but also to break-up its shape from the air. The soldier on the right appears to be part of the *Gebirgsjäger* or mountain troops.

An interesting photograph showing three Pz.Kpfw.I. Ausf.B's making there way along a road in the hilly forested area of the Ardennes in May 1940. The vehicle leading the drive is a Pz.Kpfw.II. There was approximately 640 Pz.Kpfw.I's dispersed throughout the ten Panzer divisions. These vehicles belonged *Panzergruppe Kleist*, whose force was to carry out the main breakthrough operation on the Meuse River.

A Panzer commander in the turret of his Pz.Kpfw.I.Ausf.B poses for the camera with a smile during Germany's furious drive through France. Although the armoured spearhead through the Low Countries and France had been a complete success, it was in France that the Pz.Kpfw.I was totally outmoded as a battle tank.

A Pz.Kpfw.I.Ausf.B hidden in some undergrowth during the opening phase of the invasion of Russia in June 1941. By this period of the war, the Pz.Kpfw.I's days were numbered. During the opening attacks of 'Barbarossa' this light, thinly armoured vehicle was used to fill the units of the Panzer divisions, for the *Panzerwaffe* still lacked sufficient heavy armour.

Sunk in a morass of mud. Although this was a common occurrence in the vast sprawling wastelands of the Soviet Union, the Pz.Kpfw.I was generally unable to move from the quagmire, and frequently became immobile. The crew were therefore compelled to wait for a towing tractor, which sometimes took a considerable amount of time. This scene was repeated time and time again in the autumn of 1941.

A Pz.Kpfw.I.Ausf.B races through the snow during winter operations in Russia in late 1941. By early the following year the Pz.Kpfw.I was finally taken out of service and given to the police and anti-partisan units. They were still used for training purposes and remained an excellent training tank until the end of the war.

A Pz.Kpfw.I.Ausf.B with its commander preparing to climb inside the tank. Even in Russia the Ausf.B model did not fare much better from the Ausf.A. When the larger heavier Russian tanks began appearing on the battlefield losses among these light Panzers were immense.

# Chapter Three

# Panzerkampfwagen.II

With the suspension of further development of the Pz.Kpfw.I, the *Panzerwaffe* were left with the larger light tank to mass-produce, the *Panzerkampfwagen.II* or Pz.Kpfw.II. It entered service due to the delay of the *Panzerkampfwagen.III* and IV, which both were more powerful and had a much larger gun. The Pz.Kpfw.II went into production in 1935. The first variants consisted of the Ausf.a1, a2, and a3, which had small modifications of the engine and cooling system. There were only a few of these variants produced. Some were tested in the Spanish Civil War.

In 1937 the Ausf.C became the main prototype with a brand new leaf spring suspension system with its familiar running gear of five large disc type road wheels. From thereafter the Ausf.C was used not only as the lead combat Panzer, but also as a training vehicle as well. A crew of three manned the light tank: the commander/gunner, loader/operator and driver. Maximum recommended speed in the six forward gears was: 1st – 5kph; 2nd –10kph; 3rd – 12kph; 4th – 21kph; 5th – 30kph; 6th – 40kph. Levers operating a clutch and brake mechanism that effected the steering of the vehicle. Its main armament was a 2cm cannon with a co-axle 7.92mm MG34 machine gun. The 2cm cannon was fired from a trigger on the elevating hand wheel to the commander's left, and the MG34 from a trigger on the traverse hand wheel to his right. Inside the fighting compartment there was no less than 18 magazines containing 180 rounds for the 2cm cannon. For the MG34 there were a total of 17 belt bags containing 2,550 rounds. Keeping the rounds free from dust and dirt was always a problem for the tank crews and this frequently led to jamming in the weapons feed mechanism. In sandy and dusty environments Panzer crews usually stuffed greaseproof paper into the mouth of the belt bag, keeping the rounds free from contamination with the dusty air.

Crews continued to train extensively with the Ausf.C, which soon became known as the 'fast combat wagon'. But still designers were determined to re-develop the vehicle.

In May 1938 the Ausf.D and Ausf.E appeared with another new suspension. But soon, these two variants proved unsuccessful and were taken out of service following an unsatisfactory performance. The *Panzerwaffe* were thus left with the

Ausf.C, which in spite being underpowered, under-gunned and with thin armoured plating, it was the backbone of the Panzer divisions of the early Blitzkrieg campaigns.

Throughout 1939 and 1940 the Ausf.C continued to receive modifications. In September 1939 it saw its debut against Poland with some 1, 223 Pz.Kpfw.II's distributed among the armoured formations. In total there were 78 Pz.Kpfw.II's lost during the Polish campaign. The new tried and tested Blitzkrieg strategy of warfare owed much to the German light tanks, in spite them being intended primarily for training and light reconnaissance work. The vast majority of machines making up the striking force of the Panzer divisions in Poland were the Pz.Kpfw.I and Pz.Kpfw.II.

The following year the Pz.Kpfw.II was again embroiled in heavy action, this time against the Low Countries and France. Yet again the vehicles deficient firepower and protection was masked to some extent by another easy victory. Out of the 825 Pz.Kpfw.II's that attacked the West in the summer of 1940, only ten per cent were lost.

The success of the Pz.Kpfw.II led to another variant, the Ausf.F entering service in early 1941. It was protected by 35mm frontal armour and 20mm side armour. The series continued with the Ausf.G and Ausf.J, which were distinguished from the Ausf.F by addition of a stowage bin to the turret rear. Production of these models did not stop until as late as 1944.

When the Germans finally attacked Russia in the summer of 1941 the high losses in light tanks demonstrated that the Pz.Kpfw.II was so under-gunned and under-armoured that it could not fight effectively on the Eastern Front. But the Germans still continued with production of the Ausf.F, Ausf.G and Ausf.J. By late 1942 the majority of these vehicles were performing scouting missions during bitter fighting. By the following year it seemed destined that all the light tanks would have been withdrawn from service. However, remarkably, in 1943 another variant entered service under the designation Pz.Kpfw.II (Sd.Kfz.123) Ausf.L. It was later amended to *Panzerspahwagen.II Luchs* or Lynx. Only 100 of these tanks were completed and the 9.Panzer-Division was the only division to receive them. Technically the Lynx was an armoured reconnaissance vehicle, and it was used exclusively by armoured reconnaissance battalions. Plans for a more heavily armoured Lynx with a 5cm gun and MG42 machine gun version was subsequently cancelled. Had this tank been built, it would have been known as the *Leopard*.

By the end of 1941 it was all too obvious that the usefulness of the Pz.Kpfw.II as a gun tank was at its end. What followed was a number of converted variants using leftover chassis's that served as suitable mountings for its first generation tank destroyers. Among them were the *Wespe* and *Marder.II*, an artillery observation tank, recovery vehicle, ammunition carrier and a number of other small converted vehicles.

As for the Pz.Kpfw.II tank itself, the Eastern Front had been its swan song of the early encounters with the Russian T-34's. Symbolically, the departure of the light tank as a front line fighting weapon was accompanied by that of General Heinz Guderian, the arbiter of early German tank warfare. Much larger and deadlier tanks were now needed to stem the rout in Russia. These would be known as the main battle tanks of the war, and with it a new generation of vehicles and converted tank destroyers would be deployed to face an ever-increasing challenge on the battlefield.

A Pz.Kpfw.II. Ausf.C on a training exercise in 1938. This vehicle was powered by a Maybach HL 62 TRM carburetted six cylinder engine. Its running gear consisted of 2 tracks with 108 links each with five medium sized road wheels in line, four return rollers with five quarter-elliptic springs.

A column of Pz.Kpfw.II. Ausf.C`s during a military procession. The Ausf.C first appeared in 1937 and saw an increase in frontal armour thickness from 14.5mm to 30mm. This was also the first vehicle of the series to be introduced with the five-wheel quarter-elliptical leaf spring suspension for which this vehicle is generally remembered.

A Pz.Kpfw.II whilst operating on the Eastern Front during the early autumn of 1941 crosses a stream. The vehicle is painted in overall dark grey and displays the tactical number '42', which has been painted in white on the side of the turret. Note the unofficial 'Ghost Division' insignia of the 11.Panzer-Division painted in yellow on the side of the vehicles plate.

The commander of a Pz.Kpfw.II. Ausf.C receives the salute from soldiers and officers during a military procession. The Commander-in-Chief of the *Wehrmacht* General Walter von Brauchitsch takes the salute.

A Pz.Kpfw.II moves along one of the many dirt roads that connected Poland from west to east during the September campaign of 1939. The tank commander can be seen waving at the camera as his Panzer moves past smouldering buildings. Note the old style national cross-painted in black with a thick white outline.

A Pz.Kpfw.II and Pz.Kpfw.III rest in a field during a lull in the fighting in the French campaign in May 1940. Both vehicles are painted in overall dark grey. The Pz.Kpfw.II has either the number `121` or `124` painted in yellow on the rear of the vehicle, just above the exhaust cowling. Note the numbers of jerry cans stowed onboard the engine deck.

A Pz.Kpfw.II during a training exercise demonstrates its power and versatility by driving through a building. In order to protect its armament the 2cm cannon and MG34 machine have been removed. The vehicles maximum speed was 40 kph with a road range of some 200km.

During the invasion of France in May 1940 a group of Pz.Kpfw.II's from the 1.Panzer-Division arrive at the Channel coast. The 1.Panzer-Division consisted of two Panzer regiments 1 and 2. In each regiment there contained some 100 Pz.Kpfw.II's. This was the largest contingent of any one type of Panzer model in the entire division.

A Pz.Kpfw.II has halted near a railway crossing. It appears that a vehicle has been struck by one of the two locomotives on the crossing. This photograph was taken during the invasion of France in May 1940. One of the crewmembers is standing on the tank planning on his next course of action of how to get past.

The three-man crew of a Pz.Kpfw.II have paused on a road for a break during Panzer Regiment.33's furious advance through France. Panzer-Regiment.33 was part of the 9.Panzer-Division. Although the weakest division in the field it was equipped with two battalions, consisting of some 75 Pz.Kpfw.II's.

Two Pz.Kpfw.II's advance along a road during the invasion of France. Both the Pz.Kpfw.I and Pz.Kpfw.II still represented the substantial majority among the Panzers fighting in the West. There were some 1,478 light tanks fielded against the French and British Expeditionary Force. However, the French Army alone could deploy some 3,000 tanks, many of which were better armed and better protected than the best German Panzers.

A Pz.Kpfw.II has moved along a railway track within striking distance of a mountain tunnel. Two soldiers can be seen onboard the engine deck, whilst one of the tank men tends to his vehicle, making sure everything is secure. As the war progressed more and more infantry utilised the tank as a form of transportation to one part of the battlefield to another.

Pz.Kpfw.II's advance along a road during the invasion of Russia in 1941. Even when the Germans unleashed their mighty Panzer force against the Red Army they still had preponderance of light tanks. These light Panzers formed the principal armament of 6., 7., 8., 12., 19. and 20. Panzer divisions. Altogether 17 Panzer divisions, with two more in reserve, spearheaded the invasion, organised into four *Panzergruppen*.

A Pz.Kpfw.II. Ausf.F moves quickly along a typical road in the Soviet Union. Although this Panzer was deemed the stopgap weapon in the *Panzerwaffe*, even in 1941 it was still the most numerous vehicle to see action in the Panzer divisions.

The crew of a Pz.Kpfw.II. pose for the camera with some infantry during a brief pause in operations in Russia in the summer of 1941. At this stage of the war Panzer crews still felt invincible against their enemy, in spite of the predominant amount of light tanks being used to spearhead the advance. The worst was still to come.

Two Pz.Kpfw.II's move across a field during summer operations in Russia in 1941. Unlike France, where the strategic objective was just mechanically attainable, in Russia where objectives much were further away, and the majority of the drive was done off road, the light Panzers consequently found the going very difficult indeed.

A Pontoon bridge section has been utilised into ferrying two Pz.Kpfw.II's across a river in Russia. Although this was sometimes the quickest method of transportation of heavy armour, crossing an expanse of water could be very dangerous too. With no cover, it was exposed to direct and indirect fire, and if the enemy did not kill you, there was always a prospect of drowning.

A Pz.Kpfw.II flanked by two Pz.Kpfw.III's during a fierce attack on a town in Russia in the summer of 1941. A column of Sd.Kfz.251 halftracks can be seen moving along the road, probably carrying motorized infantry as support.

A Pz.Kpfw.II has halted inside a town during partisan operations in the Balkans in 1941. Although this period saw the light tanks being used extensively in Russia, because of their infectiveness on the front lines, they were also used for reconnaissance duties and in an anti-partisan role.

A number of Panzer variants consisting of Pz.Kpfw.II's, III's and IV's on the battlefield in the summer of 1941. The vehicles have been purposely spaced apart in order to reduce the chances of aerial attack destroying large parts of the armoured spearhead.

Pioneers watch as a Pz.Kpfw.II. crosses a pontoon bridge in Russia in 1942. Foliage can be seen attached to the rear of the vehicle. By this period of the war the light tanks were already dwindling in quantity due to high losses sustained against heavier enemy armour like the T-34 tank.

A Pz.Kpfw.II. Ausf.D negotiates a narrow pontoon bridge. By winter of 1941 the future of the light ta was nearing its end was suggested that Panzers with less th 7.5cm main armame could not hope to survive on the Easte Front. What also ma it difficult for these tanks were the vast distances in which t had to travel. This w causing considerable strain on the engine and mechanical breakdowns.

A soldier sitting on a Pz.Kpfw.II poses for the camera during the winter of 1941. By this period of the war in Russia the Panzer spearheads had been eroded to mere shadows of their former selves. The autumn rains had created a sea of mud, followed by one of the worst winters ever recorded. It now left Panzers paralysed in the snow with badly demoralised crews deserting their machines before they froze in the artic wastelands.

A Pz.Kpfw.II.Ausf.L 'Luchs' or 'Lynx' leading a heavy armoured troop through the snow in 1943. These were very rare Pz.Kpfw.II vehicles and only 100 of them were ever produced. They were assigned to the 4.Panzer-Division, but the 9.Panzer-Division was the only other unit to receive a full company.

A Pz.Kpfw.II in a reconnaissance role in late 1941. In spite of the snow the vehicle has not received an application of winter whitewash paint. This is owing to the fact that the *Wehrmacht* had predicted that war in Russia would be won by October 1941, and the need for winter supplies had not been envisaged. By the following year virtually all Panzers had received some kind of winter camouflage scheme.

A Pz.Kpfw.II.Ausf.L 'Lynx' during operations in the summer of 1943. This Panzer is a company commander's vehicle and is fitted with the FuG12 radio set and star antenna. The rest of these late variants were equipped with the StuG Spr.Gerf, which replaced the FuG Spr.Ger.a radio set in 1943.

Here a column of Pz.Kpfw.II. Ausf.L 'Lynx' on a reconnaissance mission driving along one of the many dusty, sandy roads that covered hundreds of square miles of the Soviet Union.

A Pz.Kpfw.II.Ausf.L 'Lynx' company commander's vehicle in the summer of 1943. Track links have been attached to the front of the tank in order to bolster its armoured protection. Virtually all the Ausf.L variants that saw service during this period of the war had extra armoured plating fitted.

A Pz.Kpfw.II Ausf.L 'Lynx' company commander's vehicle during the winter of 1943. Note the mounted six *Nebelwurfgerät* or smoke candle dischargers, three on each side of the turret. The smoke dischargers were used as a close defence weapon and could fire smoke projectors, signal flares and anti-personnel grenades.

The commander of a Pz.Kpfw.II Ausf.L 'Lynx' looks straight at the photographer as he drives his vehicle past along a sandy road in the summer of 1943. The vehicle is finished in overall sand with green or brown camouflage pattern painted over the entire body. The digit tactical numbering system '17' is painted probably in red.

A rare photograph showing both the crew of an Ausf.L 'Lynx' during a reconnaissance role in the summer of 1943. Although a rare vehicle, the crews like it for its speed and mobility.

# Chapter Four

# Panzerkampfwagen.38 (t)

With the German occupation of the Czechoslovakian state in 1939, 150 light Czech tanks, known as LT Vz Model 38, were seized during production. The New German authorities were impressed with the design and ordered the CKD/Prage to complete production. As soon as the Czech tanks were finished they underwent a series of trials and modifications before being approved and incorporated into the *Wehrmacht*. The light tank was known as the *Panzerkampfwagen.38* (t) or Pz.Kpfw.38 (t). It was eventually to become the most widely used and important light tank incorporated by the *Panzertruppe* during the early years of the war.

From the time of its production until 1942, the Pz.Kpfw.38 (t) had several variants of which the Ausf.A was the standard version. All the variants differed only in minor detail, such as the installation of a smoke grenade rack attached to the rear of the Ausf.B. With the Ausf.E for instance, its armoured plating was more or less doubled. The Ausf.G was the last production model before the vehicle was converted exclusively for self-propelled gun mountings.

The standard variant was driven by a 125hp Praga EPA six-cylinder water cooled-engine, which produced a maximum speed of 42kph: on later models the engine was fitted with twin burrettors, which raised the output to 150kph and a top speed of 48kph. The engine was mounted in the rear of the hull and drove the tank through a transmission with five forward gears and one reverse gear. It drove a forward drive sprocket; with the track running under four rubber tyre road wheels and back over a rear idler and two track return rollers. The wheels were mounted on a leaf-spring bogie mounted on two axles. In spite of its design the suspension was extremely hard, jerky, and very unpredictable across rough terrain.

The hull and turret construction was the improved Skoda A7 3.7cm, known to the Germans as the KwK 37 (t). It was a semi automatic falling block weapon that fired AP shot at a muzzle velocity of 750 metres per second. The vehicle stowed mainly in the bulge at the turret rear ninety rounds of 3.7cm and 2,700 rounds of machine gun ammunition. The radio was mounted on the hull wall to the left of the bow gunner. The standard Pz.Kpfw.38 (t) could quickly be converted to a command role by installing radios and fitting a frame antenna above the engine deck. The command vehicle would be known in the field as *Panzerbefehlswagen*.38 (t).

Altogether 1,414 Pz.Kpfw.38 (t) s were built. Panzer crews and mechanics found the vehicle reliable and easy to work with. However, littler thought or consideration had gone into the design of the fighting compartment for the three-man crew. The commander/gunner had plenty of room, as did the hull gunner. But the loader's position was very cramped and uncomfortable.

When war finally broke out in Poland in September 1939 there were some 112 Pz.Kpfw.38 (t) s that made their debut on the battlefield. Half these vehicles were attached with the 3.Light-Division. The Czech built tanks made a very impressive entry into the war and helped spearhead the armoured thrust towards Warsaw. Losses were minimal and mechanical breakdowns were higher than expected, which in some areas hindered the drive. But overall the campaign to conquer Poland had been a complete success, with victory being achieved at a much faster pace and with few losses than had been predicted.

For the battle of France there were some 264 Pz.Kpfw.38 (t)'s used in May 1940. These vehicles were distributed between some of the most powerful Panzer divisions. Even General Erwin Rommel himself received a number of them in his 7.Panzer-Divison, declaring that they were the *Wehrmacht's* best light tanks.

Following the defeat of France Hitler turned his attention to the Soviet Union. This would be the largest contingent of Pz.Kpfw.38 (t)'s ever to see action in one theatre of war, with 623 of these Czech built vehicles poised for attack in June 1941. Although this number seemed impressive, the Panzer divisions opening the invasion of Russia were much weaker in numbers than their predecessors of 1939 and 1940, and relied heavily on the lighter tanks to provide the armoured punch. Consequently, by late summer of 1941 this put an increasing strain on the light tanks and caused a high percentage to develop mechanical problems. The Red Army too was beginning to fight back and the light tanks began to meet a significant number of new T-34 and KV-1 tanks. The Pz.Kpfw.38 (t) was no match against this new superior enemy armour, and losses grew to staggering proportions.

By 1942 the Czech light tank was finally relegated to second line duties. The Germans then began the usual process of adapting the chassis for other purposes commencing with the *Marder.III, Flakpanzer*.38 (t), and later the *Jagdpanzer Hetzer*.38 (t). In 1942 and 1943 they begun removing the turrets and converting them in to driver training vehicles.

The Pz.Kpfw.38 (t) was one of the principal German tanks of the early war years; in spite it not being of German design. The vehicle had been built in Czechoslovakia. The Czech army had ordered 150 of the LT Vz 38 light tank with a 3.7cm cannon in 1938, but the German annexation of Bohemia and Moravia a few months later saw the German Army take over the factories and complete the tank order for themselves.

A dusty Pz.Kpfw.38 (t) on a congested road during operations on the Eastern Front in the summer of 1941. Stowed on board the rear of the vehicle are a bundle of sticks. These were used to aid the tank in muddy terrain by placing them under the tracks in order to provide traction.

A rare photograph showing a Pz.Kpfw.38 (t) on a training exercise in southern Germany in early 1939. This vehicle was similarly armed and armoured to the other Czech designed model, the Pz.Kpfw.35 (t) and was driven by a 125 hp Praga six-cylinder water-cooled engine which produced a maximum speed of 42 kph: on later variants the engine was fitted with twin carburettors which raised the output to 150hp and the top speed to 48 kph.

A Pz.Kpfw.38 (t) has halted along a road prior to military operations in Poland in September 1940. The vehicle was designed for a four-man crew. The commander's cupola contained four episcopes, and immediately forward of this was a panoramic periscope.

Leaving the barracks a Pz.Kpfw.38 (t) on manoeuvres in the summer of 1940. The main armament of this vehicle was the improved Skoda A7 3.7cm cannon, known in German service as the KwK 37 (t). It was a semi-automatic falling block weapon that fired AP shot muzzle velocity of 750 metres per second and could penetrate 3.2cm of armour at 1,100 metres.

On manoeuvres a Pz.Kpfw.38 (t) moves along a dusty road. Altogether this Czech designed tank ran to several variants of which the Ausf.A was the standard version taken over at the time of occupation of Czechoslovakia. Most of the models only differed in minor detail, such as the installation of a smoke grenade rack at the rear of the Ausf.B, whilst the Ausf.E armoured plating was doubled to the front and sides.

Two Pz.Kpfw.38 (t)'s advance along a road during the Polish Campaign in September 1939. Altogether 1,414 of these vehicles were built. It was reliable and easy to maintain Panzer and was used extensively in the *Panzerwaffe* to bolster the already large contingent of light tanks that were predominantly spearheading the armoured assault across Europe.

A Pz.Kpfw.38 (t) leads the advance through a Russian village in 1941. The vehicles following are a Pz.Kpfw.II. Ausf.C and a Pz.Kpfw.IV. Although lightly armoured the Pz.Kpfw.38 (t) was able to easily use its mobility to outflank the ponderous and antiquated Polish tanks and destroy them.

A Pz.Kpfw.38 (t) has halted at the roadside. The flag attached from the tanks turret indicates that it has either broken down or in need of some kind of assistance. Curious soldiers on bicycles have stopped, indicating that the crew are obviously not with their vehicle.

A column of Pz.Kpfw.38 (t)'s advance through a French town in May 1940. The crew are wearing Zeltbahn or waterproof shelter triangle capes issued to the *Wehrmacht*. This form of waterproof protective clothing was not used very widely by Panzer crews for the cape was difficult to manoeuvre inside the small confines of the tank.

Advancing along a road somewhere in northern France in May 1940. The Pz.Kpfw.38 (t) was able to use its speed and firepower with total effect against the French and the British Expeditionary Force. The 38 (t) were able to penetrate the enemy tanks weaker side armour and tracks and score a number of sizable kills.

In a French village a Pz.Kpfw.38 (t) has fallen foul to enemy anti-tank gunners, which have brought the Panzer to a flaming halt. An anti-tank shell has penetrated the vehicles side with such considerable force it has immobilized it by blowing apart its track links. Black scorched marks over the wheels and hull suggest the vehicle may have had an internal fire. The survival of the crew is unknown.

A Pz.Kpfw.38 (t) rolls along a road in Russia in the early weeks of the campaign in July 1941. The Panzer commander is dressed in the familiar black Panzer uniform and the new Panzer field cap. Note the crews steel helmets attached to the tanks turret.

A Pz.Befw.38 (t) command vehicle passes a long column of dejected Russian PoWs. Their fait can only be imagined. By this time of the war the 38 (t) was largely obsolete as a combat vehicle, being only able to deal with lighter Soviet tanks.

One of the most costly parts of the war in Russia during the victorious months of 'Barbarossa' was the amount of light tanks that were knocked out by Soviet anti-tank gunners. This Pz.Kpfw.38 (t) has been put out of action. The tactical number '811' is painted in red with a thick white outline. These large bright tactical numbers were easy targets to well trained enemy anti-tank gunners.

A Pz.Kpfw.38 (t) advances along a road during the height of the summer in Russia in August 1941. The dust clouds created by the tanks tacks and exhaust was more than enough to rouse the awareness of Soviet fighters. Note one of the crewmembers is wearing aviator goggles to protect his eyes from the dust.

Total devastation on a road in Russia. These Pz.Kpfw.38 (t)'s have more than likely been attacked by Soviet aircraft. On the road to Moscow alone the *Panzerwaffe* reported the complete loss of 86 percent of the Pz.Kpfw.38 (t). These losses were so high that this light Czech tank was never able to recover, and consequently were phased out the following year.

A Pz.Kpfw.38 (t) wades across a river during the initial phase of Operation Typhoon, the failed assault on Moscow. In total there were some 623 of the Czech Panzers that saw action on the Eastern Front. The bulk of them were used to spearhead the central drive through the heart of the Soviet Union and the final attack on Moscow that began in September 1941.

The crew of a Pz.Kpfw.38 (t) pose for the camera during the French campaign with two motorcyclists wearing the familiar motorcycle rubbersized coat. The tank is painted in overall dark grey and the large tactical numbers `621` are painted in yellow on the side of the turret. The 38 (t) were well liked among the crews it served and scored a number of successful engagements during the French campaign. However, even by this early period of the war it was deemed obsolete. The campaign in Russia the following year would be the deciding factor. .

Troops support a 38 (t) as it crosses one of the many anti-tank trenches that were frantically dug by civilians across large areas of Western Russia. Along the entire front the Panzers were ordered to drive forward into the Russian heartlands with its mechanised forces, thus exposing them to danger of substantial losses in men and material.

German troops dismount from a Pz.Kpfw.38 (t) as it begins to experience problems driving through mud. This was one major problem that hindered Panzer crews during their advance through Russia. A brief downpour could suddenly turn a road into a quagmire of mud and water. Wheeled vehicles quickly became stuck, compelling tracked vehicles to tow them out of difficulty.

A 38 (t) crew pause during its the advance on Moscow in early October 1941. Even by the time the operation to attack the Soviet capital was ordered all German armoured front line formations were well below strength. The light tanks alone averaged between 25 percent and 50 percent down on losses.

A Pz.Kpfw.38 (t) advances along a road ahead of a Pz.Kpfw.IV during the summer of 1941. Attached to the 38 (t) is a Panzer signal flag. The meaning of the coloured flags and pennants varied from time to time and according to the manner in which they were displayed. Some were used to indicate that they had taken up position, whilst another meant 'follow me' or that it had broken down.

In the depths of the Russian winter in December 1941. Here a Pz.Kpfw.38 (t) is towing a support vehicle along a muddy road during Operation Typhoon. Canvas sheeting has been draped over the machine gun and main armament in order to protect it from dirt and harsh climate.

A Pz.Kpfw.38 (t) in January 1942 has received an application of winter white wash camouflage paint. Note the predominate use of horse drawn transport. Due the lack of motor vehicles the *Wehrmacht* was dependent on nearly 1,000,000 horses. However, some 1,000 of the animals died each day on average during the war in Russia.

The crew of a Pz.Kpfw.38 (t) pose for the camera in early 1942. By this period of the war the ever-increasing demand to replenish the *Panzerwaffe* with heavier Panzers was eventually to see the relegation of the 38 (t) to second-line duties. Whilst it fought its last battles on the Eastern Front designers began the usual process of adapting the chassis for other purposes and up-gunning the firing capabilities of the old machines.

# Chapter Five

# Panzerkampfwagen.III

When designers planned to develop the *Panzerkampfwagen.III* or Pz.Kpfw.III they envisaged on producing a vehicle that would be the *Wehrmacht's* main battle tank. It was Daimler-Benz that built the first prototype in 1936 and secretly developed it as a *Zugführerwagen* or Platoon commander's truck. Although the designers seriously considered installing a 5cm gun it would of meant an extensive re-design programme, so a smaller 3.7cm gun was used instead.

In 1937 following various modifications, the first variant, the Ausf.A, rolled out of production, and by the end of the year, 15 were produced. Only 8 of the variants, however, were fully armed. All the unarmed tanks were used for further modifications and various other tests.

Whilst the Ausf.A was being modified Daimler-Benz produced 15 Ausf.B's and 15 Ausf.C's. These two variants were completed for trials by early 1938. During 1938 the next variant, the Ausf.D, was developed, 55 of which were produced in 1939. Of the entire production run, only 30 Ausf.D's were armed.

All the early Pz.Kpfw.III variants were pre-prototypes and unsuited for large-scale production. Every new prototype variant that was developed was slightly improved from the last model. Only a relatively small number of Ausf.D's actually saw combat during the early part of the war. In fact, there were only 98 of them deployed for active service during the Polish campaign. There success, however, could not properly be monitored for they were up against antiquated enemy armour. By early 1940 the Ausf.D was handed over for training purposes.

The first Pz.Kpfw.III variant to go into anything like full-scale production was the Ausf.E. With thicker frontal armour, and a Maybach HL 120TR engine and new suspension and gearbox, the Ausf.E was far superior to any other variant in its class so far produced. By 1940, and during the Ausf.E production, it was decided to fit all the variants with a 5cm gun as standard. In April 1940, the Ausf.G entered service and was armed with the more powerful 5cm KwK L/42 gun.

One month later in the West the new up-gunned Pz.Kpfw.III unleashed its might against the Low Countries and France. Some 456 of them were dispersed among the Panzer divisions and were the third largest contingent of armour in the *Wehrmacht.*

The primary task of the Pz.Kpfw.III was intended to fight other tanks. But although it was a well-built tank, in terms of armour, armament and mobility, it was not outstanding. It was, however, influential in having a three-man turret crew (gunner, loader and commander) leaving the commander free to concentrate on commanding the tank and maintaining situational awareness.

Following the victory over France production of the Pz.Kpfw.III increased, and by February 1941, some 450 Ausf.G variants had left the assembly lines and made ready for service. During early 1941, German factories had built another variant the Ausf.H that had received additional all-round armoured plating. The subsequent variant was the Ausf.J. A few hundred of them featured bolted 5cm frontal armour, while the remainder were fitted with the new potent long-barrelled 5cm KwK 39 L/60 gun. In total there were some 2,516 of these variants produced between March 1941 and July 1942.

During the opening stages of the invasion of the Soviet Union in June 1941, there were some 956 Pz.Kpfw.III's. This was by far the largest contingent of armour to fight in the war thus far. Although the Pz.Kpfw.III made staggering successes the eventual distances, which had to be covered, limited its tactics, as well as causing breakdowns and immense supply problems.

Whilst the battles on the Eastern Front continued to rage, between June and December 1942, the Ausf.L made its debut and featured the same powerful KwK 39 L/60 gun as the Ausf.J. Late that same year the Ausf.M entered service and February 1943 some 292 of them had been built. The Ausf.M was a very successful variant and incorporated a number of modifications to its chassis, including the introduction of side-skirting armoured plating or *Schürzen*. The *Schürzen* was intended primarily to protect the wheels and tracks from hollow-charge anti-tank weapons. The last variant to be produced was the Ausf.N. It was armed with a potent 7.5cm KwK L/24 gun that was previously mounted on the *Panzerkampfwagen.IV*. This vehicle was designed for heavy close-fire support and was eventually nicknamed the *Sturmpanzer.III*. In total some 666 of these variant types were built until production ceased in late 1943.

Throughout its service the Pz.Kpfw.III had shown its worth on the battlefield, in particular during the early phase of the war and the first months of Operation Barbarossa. However, against formidable Russian armour such as the T-34 medium and the KV-1 heavy tanks, the Pz.Kpfw.III was soon recognized as an inadequate weapon. By 1943 the vehicle was relegated from the Panzer divisions to training units. Only a handful of them were ever to see combat again. In the last desperate year of the war the Pz.Kpfw.III were seen in Normandy, Arnhem, northern Italy, northern Russia and the last defence of the Baltic States in early 1945.

The crew of a Pz.Kpfw.III. Ausf.E wait for a recovery unit during operation in France in May 1940. The condition of the suspension (missing front road wheel and broken track) indicates that the Panzer may have struck by a mine. Note the French prisoners walking towards the tank.

A Pz.Kpfw.III. guided by a large number of troops carefully negotiates the narrow confines of a pontoon bridge. The vehicle has no machine guns fitted, which suggests it may be on a training exercise. The Pz.Kpfw.III was the first modern main battle tank, possessing features that are still seen on tanks to this day.

On a training exercise is a group Pz.Kpfw.III's. Although the Pz.Kpfw.III was intended to be the *Wehrmacht's* main combat vehicle, from the beginning however the main armament fitted made the tank seriously undergunned. A 3.7cm cannon with a co-axial MG34 had been mounted in the first variants, Ausf.A, B, C, D and E: 'E' being the 1939 production model.

Soldiers and crew pose on the turret of a Pz.Kpfw.III. Ausf.E. Note that lengths of track have been stored on the surface of the vehicle as extra protection against enemy anti-tank fire. The Ausf.E was the first real production model, and ran on torsion bars, which would be standard suspension for the rest of the series. The hullside were now made of single plates, which featured escape hatches for the driver and radio operator.

Solders pose with a Pz.Kpfw.III.AusF. This variant featured a new ignition system, and cast air intakes were added to the hull front to cool the tanks brakes. About 100 of these models were built with a 5cm gun. The armoured plating was increased to 30mm.

A group of soldiers and Panzer crew pose for the camera at the side of a road whilst a long column of Pz.Kpfw.III's rest during manoeuvres. This type of tank formation in long columns would of proved fatal during military operations and an easy target to enemy fighters.

During the early days of the invasion of Russia in the summer of 1941. Three Pz.Kpfw.III's can be seen moving along a dusty road with a Pz.Kpfw.II. Motorcycle combinations and a Horch light cross-country car support the drive. In the opening attack against the Soviet Union a total of 965 Pz.Kpfw.III's were employed on the front lines.

A Pz.Kpfw.III. Ausf.H, during a military parade in 1942. The Panzer has a new cupola added to the turret, as was a circular vent on its roof. The vehicle is fitted with a 5cm KwK38 L/42 cannon with a co-axial MG34 for local defence.

During the same military parade in 1942 the commander of a Pz.Kpfw.III Ausf.H takes the salute as his vehicle rolls past. The visible marking on the Panzer next to the driver's visor is a yellow inverted 'Y' with a single vertical stroke. This represents that the vehicle belongs to the 2.Panzer-Division, after 1941.

A Pz.Kpfw.III undergoing maintenance in a field workshop. The mechanics are more than likely working on the tanks engine as a portal crane is visible near the engine deck. The Pz.Kpfw.III in the main was a reliable machine, however, the long distances in which it had to travel put a big strain of the vehicles mechanical parts.

A Pz.Kpfw.III advances along a muddy road during the summer of 1941. Even a short downpour could make these roads in Russia impassable for most wheeled as well as tracked vehicle traffic. This particular road has been damaged by the constant cross-country movement of tracked vehicles.

The crew of a Pz.Kpfw.III pose for the camera during the winter of 1941. With no provisions for winter warfare both the crew and the tank have not received any type of winter protection. By early 1942, when it seemed the war would continue through the year, winter white wash paint was widely incorporated into the Panzer camouflage scheme.

A Pz.Kpfw.III rests in front of a building in Russia during the failed assault on Moscow in December 1941. A thin layer of snow sits on the tank suggesting that the crew are resting and probably keeping warm inside the building. By this period of the war Panzers in Army Group Centre had become frozen in snowdrifts in temperatures 40 below zero.

A knocked out Pz.Kpfw.III. Ausf.E awaits recovery by workshop units. The Panzer appears to be the victim of mines of large calibre artillery, as the photograph suggests a large explosion has ripped clean off the offside track. There is also damage to the skirting as well where most of the impact was received.

A Pz.Kpfw.III rests in the western desert in 1941. The vehicle is armed with a 3.7cm cannon and MG34 machine gun for local defence. Note the Afrika palm tree symbol painted on the left front beneath the machine gun. These vehicle insignia were generally painted in white or yellow on the front glacis plate and rear hull of tanks, on the front and rear fenders of soft skinned vehicles.

The crew of a Pz.Kpfw.III wait in the hot baking sun of the North African desert whilst a field maintenance workshop team undergo repairing the Panzers engine. The Pz.Kpfw.III as a whole was a robust and reliable tank and was used extensively in the North African Campaign between 1941 and 1943.

The commander of a *Befehls* Panzer.III.Ausf.E surveyors the Russian steppes with his Zeiss binoculars. The *Befehlspanzer* is recognizable by the frame antenna, which can just be seen attached to the rear of the vehicles superstructure. The 3.7cm KwK L/46.5 cannon is probably a dummy mounting.

A Pz.Kpfw.III. Ausf.J fitted with a short-barrelled 5cm KwK L/42 gun, passes through a burning Russian village. Because the *Wehrmacht* were totally unprepared for the winter conditions in the East and did not have enough supplies of washable winter camouflage paint, the crews frequently improvised. Here in this photograph the crew have used chalk to help conceal the vehicle against the artic terrain.

The crew of a Pz.Kpfw.III. Ausf.J take immediate precautions by waving and displaying a national flag as they identify a German aircraft approaching their position. During 1941 and early 1942 Panzer crews often carried the national flag for aerial recognition. However, as the war progressed the flags were disbanded, as they became easy target to Soviet anti-tank gunners.

A Pz.Kpfw.III has developed a mechanical failure and broken down outside a forest somewhere in western Russia. The crew from a maintenance company have already secured the vehicle with a tow bar in order to take it away to a workshop. At nearly 23 tons towing rope or chains were simply inadequate to tow the tank, especially along some of the uneven roads.

A Pz.Kpfw.III. Ausf.J in the early spring of 1942 armed with a 5cm cannon. A few hundred of these variants featured bolted 5cm frontal armour, while subsequent Ausf.J models mounted very powerful long-barrelled 5cm KwK 39 L/60 gun. In total there were some 2,516 Ausf.J variants built between March 1941 and July 1942.

A Pz.Kpfw.III. Ausf.J has parked in front of a deserted Russian building, and appears to have been temporarily occupied by the Panzer crew. Note the shirtless Panzer crewman at the rear of the tank.

At a workshop a number of Pz.Kpfw.III Ausf.J's armed with 5cm cannons are parked in the forecourt prior to being sent back to the frontlines. The railway line suggests that these vehicles will be transported by rail, which was the quickest and safest method of moving Panzers to one part of the front to another.

A Pz.Kpfw.III.Ausf.J or L is stationary in a field whilst soldiers engage enemy troops hiding in undergrowth. Two infantrymen can be seen at the rear of the Panzer using the vehicle as cover. Foliage has been draped over the engine deck in order to afford some kind of extra camouflage.

A company-sized detachment of Pz.Kpfw.Ausf.J or L move along in a familiar style column across dirt roads that linked Russia from west to east. The long drives in which these vehicles had to endure quite frequently outstripped supplies and consequently brought the armoured spearheads to a standstill. The crews sometimes stood alone in the wilderness of the Russian countryside with their immobile panzer, prone to attack.

# Chapter Six

# Panzerkampfwagen.IV

The *Panzerkampfwagen*.IV or Pz.Kpfw.IV became the most popular Panzer in World War Two and remained in production throughout the war. Originally the Pz.Kpfw.IV was designed as an infantry support tank, but soon proved to be so diverse and effective that it earned a unique tactical role on the battlefield.

The prototype of the Pz.Kpfw.IV was given the code name *Bataillonführerwagen*. Krupp, MAN and Rheinmetall Borsig were ordered by Hitler to develop a prototype. The Krupp design – the VK 2001 (K) ñ was finally selected to enter full-scale production in 1935. The Ausf.A was built as a pre-production model and only 35 of them were produced. The Ausf.A weighed 17 tons and mounted a potent short-barrelled 7.5cm KwK L/24 gun. Its unique superstructure allowed the vehicle to be later modified and up-gunned. In 1938, the next variant emerged, the Ausf.B. The same year Krupp-Gruson produced the Ausf.C and 134 of this model were in production until 1939. During the same year another new variant, the Ausf.D, was introduced, featuring heavier armour.

When the *Wehrmacht* attacked Poland in September 1939, there were 211 Pz.Kpfw.IV's lined up for the attack. The following year during the battle for France the number increased only slightly to 366. After the victorious Polish and Western campaigns Hitler ordered increased production of the Pz.Kpfw.IV. This subsequently saw development of the Ausf.E. Various modifications were made to this model including thicker armour and improved vision blocks for the driver. The Ausf.E was the first of a line of variants fitted with turret mounted stowage bins. It entered service between December 1940 and March 1941. During this period, another variant was built, the Ausf.F1. This was manufactured between February 1941 and March 1942, and was in direct response to the heavier Allied tanks confronted during the Western Front campaign in 1940. Some 975 Ausf.F1's were delivered to the front lines and 548 of them were ready for action by the time orders came to unleash it's mighty forces against a bewildered Russian Army.

In mid-1942, the Ausf.F2 variant made its debut. The Panzer was up-gunned with a long barrelled 7.5cm KwK 40 L/43 gun. The vehicle was a powerful machine and was immediately transported by train to the Eastern Front to do battle against the Russian T-34 tank. In May 1942, the Ausf.F.2 was followed by the modified version of the Ausf.G with enhanced armour protection and new improved muzzle break on the 7.5cm gun. There were some 1,724 Ausf.F and Ausf.G tanks that fought on the battlefields of Russia.

The next variant to make its debut was the Ausf.H. This vehicle made its debut in April 1943. It was armed with a newer version of the 7.5cm KwK 40 L/48 gun and was fitted with Schürzen. The Ausf.H dominated the Panzer divisions in which it served and saw extensive action fighting alongside the most powerful Panzers of the war, the Tigers and Panthers. Over 3,770 of the Ausf.H models were built. These vehicles were so powerful that they actually helped support the main spearhead during the opening phase of the battle of Kursk in July 1943. Although the offensive was a complete failure the Pz.Kpfw.IV had earned the respect from both the *Wehrmacht* and *Waffen-SS* troops it helped support.

The last variant to roll off the assembly lines was the Ausf.J, which entered service in March 1944. With modified suspension and larger fuel tanks, 2,392 of these vehicles were moved to the front lines to deal with the ever-increasing threat of enemy firepower. From 1943 onwards the Pz.Kpfw.IV spearheaded the elite tank battalions and would continue its duty until the last days of the war.

Between 1936 and 1945, a total of 8,472 Pz.Kpfw.IV's were built. For the majority of the war the Pz.Kpfw.IV was certainly a match for its opponent's heavy tanks and quickly and effectively demonstrated its superiority on the battlefield. In fact it played a prominent role in the desperate attempt to halt the Soviet onslaught, and was also used with deadly effect in the West by performing defensive operations. It was an ultimate credit to the Panzer divisions it served, and was the only Panzer to stay in production throughout the war. It was also a credit to its design that there was more Pz.Kpfw.IV chassis's converted into various self-propelled anti-tank weapons than any other Panzer that entered service. Apart from the various prototype projects and the command tanks, observation vehicles, ammunitions carriers, recovery vehicles, and amphibious armoured ferry vehicles that saw service, there were a multitude of converted anti-tank and self-propelled vehicles such as the *Moblewagen, Wirbelwind, Ostwind, Nashorn, Hummel, Sturmgeschütz.IV, JagdPanzer.IV/70, Panzer-Selbstahrlafette.IVa*, and the *Sturmpanzer* IV *Brummbar*. All these specialized converted variants tried there best to counter the latest enemy tanks and hold their advance at bay.

At a workshop in Germany is a line of Pz.Kpfw.IV. Ausf.D's. This Panzer was built in the greatest quantity of any German tank and saw combat from the beginning to the end of the war. All these vehicles are attached to the 1. *Kavallerie-schützen Regiment*.11 that were part of 9.Panzer-Division and took part in operations against France in 1940.

A Pz.Kpfw.IV rolls along a road. This Panzer soon proved its worth on the battlefield and became the main battle tank during the war. The first variant came off the production line in 1936 and mounted a very powerful short-barrelled 7.5cm KwK L/24 gun. It had a unique superstructure that allowed it to be up-gunned through the war.

A Pz.Kpfw.IV advances at speed on a dirt track. The dusty vehicle has limited markings and is painted in overall dark grey. Note the spare track links attached to the front of the tank in order to increase its armoured protection. All the crew are dressed in the familiar M1934 black panzer uniform.

A Panzer commander stands next to his Pz.Kpfw.IV Ausf.D. The modifications of this variant gave it increased frontal armour, improved vision blocks for the driver, and a six speed gearbox, which enhanced its cross-country performance. This Panzer was only capable of dealing with the Soviet KV-1 and T-34 at short ranges.

At a repair depot two crewmembers stand next to their Pz.Kpfw.IV. Ausf.E. This variant entered service between December 1940 and March 1941. The tracks on the vehicle are the earlier narrow 38cm type with smooth faces on the individual links. There is a white tactical number '1' on the side of the superstructure next to the national cross, which is painted black with a white outline.

A white washed Pz.Kpfw.IV during winter operations on the Eastern Front in late 1941. During the opening attack against the Soviet Union six months earlier a total of 3,332 Panzers took part in the operation. Out of that total some 439 Pz.Kpfw.IV's were employed on the front lines, the smallest contingent of armour to see action.

A very interesting photograph showing a rare Pz.Kpfw.IV Ausf.D specially converted to operate in the English Channel for the invasion of the United Kingdom code-named 'Operation Sealion'. These Panzers were called 'Tauchpanzers' or submersible tanks. There were only a total of 48 ever manufactured. Rubbersized canvas was mounted in a number of places on the Panzer to seal the vehicle for submerged operation.

The commander of a Pz.Kpfw.IV captured on film by one of his crewmembers. The commander is wearing the short double-breasted black Panzer uniform with field cap and headphones. The uniform was specially designed to allow movement within the cramped confines of an armoured vehicle and minimizing the risk of the jacket snagging on protruding equipment.

The crew of a Pz.Kpfw.IV have halted inside a Russian town during their furious drive on the Eastern Front in the late summer of 1941. Even after two months of rapid armoured strikes and deep penetrations many of the Panzers were still driving almost unhindered along the roads.

Early 1942 and two Pz.Kpfw.IV Ausf.E's and a light Horch cross-country car have parked off the main road near some dense trees. All three vehicles have received an application of white wash winter camouflage paint..

A column of Pz.Kpfw.IV's drive across the Russian steppe. Here a crewmember takes a snap shot whilst he sits behind his commander. The road system in Russia was particular poor and where possible tank crews used the surrounding terrain in order to bypass traffic congestion or heavily urbanised areas where armoured units would be prone to attack.

A company sized detachment of Pz.Kpfw.IV. more than likely on a training ground being put through their paces against mock targets. This new variant was produced in immediate response to the heavier Allied tanks confronted during the Western campaign in 1940. Between February 1941 and March 1942, some 975 of these models were built.

A column of Pz.Kpfw.IV's rolls through the town of Tripoli in 1941. These Panzers belong to the 21.Panzer-Division. The division took part in the defensive actions against the British 'Crusader' offensive in November 1941, which virtually decimated the British 7th Armoured Brigade.

The presence of a Pz.Kpfw.IV. resting with crew has caused some interest among some infantry in the area. The Panzer is parked near some trees and the crew have utilised the surrounding foliage by attaching some of it on to the turret, just forward of the cupola.

A group of infantry equipped with bicycles pass a stationary Pz.Kpfw.IV.Ausf.F1. Seen behind is a Pz.Kpfw.IV.Ausf.2, armed with a 7.5cm KwK40 L/43. The F1. variant had increased armour over previous versions, modified turret, wider tracks and intakes on the glacis plate for brake cooling. From 1941 until 1942 these Panzers served in the Balkans, North Africa, and the Soviet Union.

A close-up view of a Pz.Kpfw.IV.Ausf.F1 during a pause in a drive through Russia in the summer of 1941. The vehicles short-barrelled KwK 37 L/24 gun can be seen along with the Notek blackout-driving headlamp and drivers visor block. Between June 1942 and July 1943, the strength of this model on the Eastern Front dropped from 208 to 60, before it was finally phased ou in the summer of 1943

A Pz.Kpfw.IV. Ausf.D attached to the 5.Panzer-Division during operations in Russia in early 1942. The driver is wearing a standard infantry greatcoat and black Panzer field cap. The vehicle is painted in winter white wash camouflage paint and bears a black national cross on the side of the chassis. Note the stowage bin unusually placed in front of the cupola.

A company of Pz.Kpfw.IV. Ausf.F or sometimes designated as the Ausf.F.2 on the Eastern Front in 1942. These vehicles have been up-gunned with a long barrelled 7.5cm KwK 40 L/43 gun and were more than capable at knocking out the Soviet T-34 tank. For additional camouflage all the Panzers have had foliage attached to the chassis and turret including parts of the barrel.

Two Pz.Kpfw.IV's Ausf.G's move along a muddy road passing a resting Pz.Kpfw.IV. Ausf.E in early 1943. The Ausf.G variant had enhanced armoured protection and improved muzzle brake on the main long barrelled 7.5cm L/48 gun. Although difficult to see both these variants have intact mounted *schürzen*.

A destroyed Pz.Kpfw.IV at the side of a road on the Eastern Front in the summer of 1943. Although it is difficult to estimate the extent of damage to the tank the vehicle looks like it has already been salvaged and lays in wait either to be reconditioned or cannibalised for spares. Note the metal clips along the trailing edge of the track guards where the *schürzen* was attached. The turret *schürzen* is also completely missing, suggesting these may have already been removed.

The crew and a commanding officer pose for the camera on board a Pz.Kpfw.IV. Ausf.G or H during the winter of 1943. Although this vehicle does not posses any *schürzen* to protect its road wheels, it does have turret *schürzen*, which was introduced in 1943. The tank is painted in winter white wash and has additional track links attached to the front of the tank to increase armoured protection.

The Bulgarian Maybach T-IV G or Pz.kpfw.IV Ausf. G belonging to the Bulgarian army. A number of armoured vehicles were sent specially from Germany to the Bulgarian army to combat and eliminate Partisan operations in the Balkans. Here the Maybach is providing transport for a group of Bulgarian soldiers.

A line of Pz.Kpfw.IV's Ausf.F2's moving along a road towards the front lines in 1943. The rear vehicle is a Pz.Kpfw.IV. Ausf.G and has intact *schürzen* mounted in a manner seen on early Panzers. The Ausf.F.2 was very successful on the Eastern Front and scored sizable kills, especially against the T-34 tank. The potent 7.5cm gun was able to penetrate 8.9cm of sloped armour at 1000m.

Another Bulgarian Maybach T-IV G. Note the red slogan that has been painted on the front of the vehicle. The slogans were intended to inspire the Panzer crews and infantry in to battle. This kind of practise was also seen extensively in the Red Army.

About to negotiate a bend on a road in the thick snow is a Pz.Kpfw.IV. The artic conditions look very severe and the Panzer crew have protected the 7.5cm gun barrel and muzzle break with canvas sheeting. Canvas sheeting is also evident just forward of the cupola attached to the turret and on the engine deck.

A Pz.Kpfw.IV. Ausf.H advances along a road in Belorussia in July 1943. The tank has intact sch͵rzen and has a three-colour camouflage scheme of brown and green over the dark sand base. Note the regimental standing white bear painted on the side of the turret. This vehicle belonged to the 3.Panzer-Division.

A Panzer crewman poses for the camera showing where a she[ll] entered the side of [a] Pz.Kpfw.IV's 7.5cm barrel. This photograph was take[n] during the opening phase of Operation Citadel, which saw th[e] largest tank battle in military history at Kursk in July 1943.

During the battle of Kursk Panzer grenadiers have removed Russian obstacles including a barbed wire entanglement in order to allow easy access for a detachment of Pz.Kpfw.IV's to pour through unhindered. The main objective of the operation was the destruction of the Red Army's massive force in the Kursk region. Once the Russian had been destroyed, the armoured force could then turn north and drive on Moscow. A very bold move for the Panzer divisions of 1943.

A destroyed Pz.Kpfw.IV. Ausf.G or H stands as a grim reminder of the savaged fighting that raged day and night in the bocage of northern France between June and August 1944. Although this vehicle may have been able to be cannibalised for spares, it is more than probable that the Panzer, like so many in this region of France, were simply abandoned after being put out of action.

A Pz.Kpfw.IV knocked out of action on the Eastern Front. Losses in Russia during 1943 had been massive. Between 1 September and 31 December 1943, all units on the Eastern Front averaged 2,000 Panzers of which only 800 were combat ready at any one time. This was a very small Panzer force for such a large front.

A decimated Pz.Kpfw.IV. Ausf.H on the Eastern Front during the winter of 1944. The vehicle has obviously received a direct hit and as a consequence of the shells impact it has blown off most of the *schürzen* plates. A thick coating of anti magnetic mine paste is evident over the chassis and turret.

A column of Maybach T-IV Pz.Kpfw.IV tanks parked on a road inside a Bulgarian town in 1944. By March 1944 the Bulgarian Army had received some 97 Pz.Kpfw.IV's from Germany. The variants they acquired mainly consisted of the Ausf.G's and some Ausf.H's, and equipped the 1st Bulgarian Tank Regiment of the 1st Armoured Brigade.

Two Pz.Kpfw.IV Ausf.H's halted in the snow in late 1944. From 1943 onwards this variant dominated the battlefield in which it served. Despite inferior numbers it fought well in western Russian and scored a great successes in a number of defensive actions in Poland.

# Chapter Seven

# Panzerkampfwagen.VI Tiger

Probably the most famous Panzer of World War Two is the *Panzerkampfwagen.IV 'Tiger.I'* or better known as the Tiger.I. It was nicknamed by the troops as the 'furniture' van, because of its sheer size. This 57-ton beast went into production in 1942, following great demands from Hitler to bolster the *Wehrmacht* and *Waffen-SS* Panzer divisions with heavier and more potent machines. Both Henschel and Porsche submitted prototypes, but Henschel was finally given the task to develop the Tiger.

The Tiger weighed some 57-tons and had very thick frontal armour. Even the side and rear armour protection was a sufficient to eliminate any serious threat from Russian 7.6cm tank guns at normal combat ranges. The tank had been fitted with a very powerful 8.8cm KwK 36 L/56 gun that were more than capable of first round hits at ranges exceeding 1000m.

The Tiger Model.E, as it was first called, was first demonstrated on Hitler's birthday in April 1942. The first production series was completed and sent to Kummersdorf the following month for testing. Delays in production were encountered due to problems with the steering gear and brakes of which both needed modifying. But the Tiger was soon being tested again and clearly demonstrated that it could withstand a lot of abuse during the test programmes.

The first Tiger's to make their combat debut on the Eastern Front was attached to the 1.*Kompanie/schwere Heeres* Panzer *Abteilung* 502. Four of them saw action around Leningrad on 29 August 1942. Originally these Tigers were supposed to be incorporated into special units with 20 heavy Panzers to be used primarily to spearhead the Panzer divisions. However, because there were not enough Tigers built the organisational concept included lighter tanks within the special heavy units. Thus the first five independent battalions that saw action in Russia would each consist on paper of nine Tigers accompanied by ten Pz.Kpfw.III's. However, by November 1942, only 13 Tigers had been built, but after that production reached 25 or more each month. From July 1942 to September 1944, when construction of the Tiger finally ceased, a total of 1,354 had rolled off the assembly lines.

The beginning of the Tigers debut on the battlefield was interrupted by many teething problems. All too often the Tiger broke down and it made it very difficult to remove the heavy tank from the battlefield. But in spite of this by 1943 independent Tiger battalions would be on hand to keep the vehicle in fighting condition.

For almost two years the Tiger saw extensive combat in Russia, North Africa, Italy and Normandy. It played a number of prominent roles in various major offensives in Russia and demonstrated its awesome killing power. At the battle of Kursk in July 1943, the Tiger was distributed among the elite *Waffen-SS* Panzer units and played a significant roll spearheading the advance through strong Russian defensive positions. By 1944 the Tiger continued to be a valuable contribution in defensive roles, both on the Eastern and Western Fronts. The skill and tenacity shown by its five man crew, together with the tanks killing power, made many Allied troops reluctant to engage the Tiger. Frequently, it took five British tanks to destroy just one Tiger. But despite its superb prowess, by August 1944 the Normandy front had almost destroyed all the remaining Tigers in the field.

With such heavy losses, the Tiger.I production was finally terminated in favour of a far superior Panzer that had just been developed by Henschel called the Pz.Kpfw.IV Ausf.B King Tiger or Tiger.II. The Tiger.II was the most formidable tank on the battlefield and possessed lethal firepower. It was armed with a potent long barrelled 8.8cm KwK 43/3 L/71 gun and for close support defence it carried two MG34 machine guns. The vehicle weighed in at a staggering 64-tons and had such superb all-round thick armoured protection it was virtually impregnable to any Allied tank.

By March 1945 some 489 Tiger.II's were produced, including 20 command variants. Despite the vehicles overwhelming firepower, it was marred on the battlefield by its sheer size and huge fuel consumption. It was also slow and lacked mobility. Consequently, the crews were compelled to use their Tiger.II in a static fire support role. However, despite its problems the tank did score a number of great tactical successes both on the Eastern and Western Fronts. They were a rare sight and only 219 of them were fielded for operations in a few of the remaining heavy tank battalions in February 1945.

Whilst the Tiger.II fought on during the last months of the war, trying to stave-off the inevitable German defeat, there was another even larger Panzer fighting in the field. It was known as the *Jagdpanzer.VI Jagdtiger* heavy tank destroyer. It was developed in 1944 as the tank destroyer counterpart to the latest tank, the Tiger.II. It was built on a Tiger.II chassis and weighed some 70-tons. It carried a six-man crew and boasted the second largest gun of any wartime tank or tank destroyer.

Only 77 *Jagdtigers* were ever delivered to the front lines. Because of disruption caused by bombing to the factories, it had affected gun production. Consequently virtually all of the *Jagdtigers* were delivered with 8.8cm anti-tank guns, instead of a

12.8cm anti-tank gun. The two units that ever received *Jagdtigers* fought on the Western Front, the former Ardennes offensive in December 1944, and later in the defence of Germany. The majority were used in their intended role as movable strong points. But the mobility in the field was restricted due to fuel shortages, mechanical breakdowns, and its sheer weight and size meant that it was unmanoeuvrable, slow and almost impossible to conceal from the air. Whilst in action the vehicle was easy prey, especially in urbanized combat. It was almost always overwhelmed by infantry with bazookas or charges that struck the most vulnerable parts, the wheels and tracks.

In spite of the huge losses sustained, the Pz.Kpfw.VI Tiger, the Tiger.II, and the massive *Jagdtiger*, all played a decisive roll in the development of the Panzer. Although the Tiger did not change the course of the war, it certainly affected the way in which the war was fought. It will undoubtedly remain forever a symbol of formidable German Panzer formations of World War Two.

The Pz.Kpfw.VI.Tiger tank was probably the most famous Panzer of World War Two. Here in this photograph a Tiger passes a destroyed Russian tank during operations in Russia in the late summer of 1943. From August 1942 to the September 1944 there were some 1,354 Tiger's built.

Two Tiger's crossing a stretch of water during operations on the Eastern Front during the early summer of 1943. The Tiger was armed with a very powerful 8.8cm KwK 36 L/56 gun and had a very accurate first round capability at ranges exceeding 1000m.

An early Tiger I is being prepared to be moved by low-loader to join its new unit on the Eastern Front. Stowed on board with the Tiger are spare road wheels and track. Attached to the turret sides are the triple smoke candle dischargers. Normally whilst being transported the gun tube had a canvas cover fitted over the muzzle break.

Another view of the same Tiger on board the heavy-duty low loading trailer. These low-loading vehicles were used widely by the special independent Tiger battalions, whose job it was to move the tanks from one place to another or recover them from the battlefield after sustaining serious damage whilst fighting.

A Tiger I in the summer of 1943. This vehicle belongs to the *Schwere* Panzer *Kompanie*, SS-Panzer Regiment 2 '*Das Reich*', in Russia. It can be identified through their unique tactical number system on the side of the turret consisting of the letter 'S' followed by the numbers designating the platoon and position within the platoon. This tank has left the factory and still carries a coat of *Feldgrau*. It would soon be repainted for the Kursk offensive in July 1943.

A Tiger.I on a training excise in 1943. The word 'Tika' painted on the vehicles front offside was a diminutive for Tiger. The Panzer belonged to the *Schwere SS-Panzer Abteilung* 102, *2.SS Panzergrenadier-Division Das Reich.* This unit was originally created in April 1943.

An early production model Tiger more than likely being driven along a road in the factory grounds, prior to being released for final approval tests. The vehicle has a full array of triple smoke launchers on the turret as well as a complete set of fenders and mud flaps, and is fitted with the *'Feifel'* air filter system on the hull rear plate. A protective covering is evident over the gun barrel muzzle break and MG34 machine gun.

Three Tigers wade across a river somewhere in Russia. These Tiger's more than likely belong to Schwere Heere's Panzer Abteilung 506. Note the number '7' painted in white on the side of the turret.

On a training exercise rests a Tiger with a crewman. The vehicles MG34 machine gun is missing, but will be re-installed prior to transportation to the front lines. The first Tigers to see action on the Eastern Front was in the attack on Leningrad in August 1942 where it was used in unsuitable terrain.

General Heinz Guderian and staff inspect a Tiger tank in 1943. One Panzer crewmember opens the commander's cupola hatch and shows the General the internal view of the commander's compartment. Guderian was the man who had formulated the concept of the tank-led *Blitzkrieg* and had transformed an outdated and depleted *Wehrmacht* into a superb armoured fighting machine.

Another photograph of General Heinz Guderian conferring with staff and a Panzer commander during an inspection of a Tiger in 1943. It was in March 1943 that Guderian was re-appointed by Hitler as Inspector General of Panzer Troops. Guderian had been given the Herculean task of repairing the losses of the *Panzerwaffe* and trying to expand the armoured force with various improvisations.

Two Tigers plough through trees on the edge of a forest in western Russia in 1943. Despite the capabilities of the Tiger and the speed in which it negotiated cross-country terrain the innovative interleaving road wheels were prone to clogging with mud, which often in winter periods froze overnight and immobilised the vehicle.

A parked Pz.Kpfw.VI Tiger I on the Eastern Front in 1943. The muzzle brake of the 8.8cm gun has been covered in order to protect it from dust and dirt. Foliage has been applied to parts of the vehicle in order to break up its distinctive shape and avoid aerial detection..

A knocked out Tiger.I. The vehicle has four spare track links attached to the side of the turret for additional armoured protection and has a thick coating of ant-magnetic mine past. The side skirts of the vehicle have been buckled in a few places suggesting that they have been caused by the enemy projectile hitting the tank.

During the early winter of 1944 a column of Tiger.I's have halted on a frozen muddy road in Russia. The Tiger crews confer about the next course of action on the battlefield. They are all wearing the white reversible camouflage smocks and the M1943 Black Panzer field cap.

In Italy a Tiger.I rests by the side of a road. The vehicle has five spare track links mounted along with one of the crews steel helmets on top of them. It has a complete set of fenders as well as mud flaps and is covered in a sandy base colour. The Tiger was committed to action in Italy with the *Schwere Panzer Abteilung* 504 and 508, I.SS.Panzer-*Korps* and a small independent unit under the name of *Tigergruppe* Meyer.

Tiger.I belonging to the *Schwere Heeres Panzer Abteilung* 508. This particular Tiger was modified with a [...]g capable of placing [...]harges. This was in [o]rder to increase the [lo]cal defence of the [ta]nk. The Tiger was [p]hotographed in Italy [n]ear the Anzio [b]ridgehead and has [m]ore than likely been [k]nocked out of [ac]tion.

A Tiger has obviously ploughed through a building and then reversed leaving the debris all over the chassis and turret. The Tiger belongs to the *Schwere* Panzer *Abteilung* 509, which was formed in September 1943. From late 1943 until the spring the following year it was engaged near Kirovograd, Kirivoi-Rog, Kiev and Pavlova in southern Russia.

Infantry have hitched a lift on board a Tiger.I of the Schwere Panzer Abteilung 503. Two other Tigers from the same unit follow the drive along an icy road. Twenty of these Tigers saw action in November and December 1942, and saw extensive fighting during the Don campaign in southern Russia.

The harsh artic weather of the Soviet Union. Here two Tiger.I's negotiate a road in a snow blizzard during operations in Russia in 1943. The Tiger is well camouflaged with a good overall application of winter whitewash paint. Note that the crew have put canvas sheeting over the barrels muzzle break in order to keep it dry and dirt free.

A pair of Panthers along with a Zug of Tiger are moving across the vast artic wasteland of the Soviet Union. At least two of the Tigers have Panzergrenadiers on board. The Panzergrenadiers were the motorized infantry and travelled by vehicle rather than on foot. They would accompany the armoured spearhead, mounted on board tanks and dismount to go into action.

A long column of Tigers moving swiftly along a road destined for the front lines in Russia in early 1944. The leading vehicle is covered with Zimmerit anti-magnetic mine paste that was ordered to be applied in August 1943. This in turn covered in a winter whitewash. Note the tow cables and track changing cables attached to the engine deck and the side of the chassis.

A Tiger.I with a liberal covering of winter whitewash over the Zimmerit anti-magnetic mine paste advances across endless Russian countryside in early 1944. Unusually along one side of the vehicle across the sand shield fenders the crew have used what appears to be barbed wire. This was obviously used to help protect the Tiger and crew from would be attackers trying to board the vehicle.

In the thick snow a dismounted Tiger crew stand next to their vehicle and inspect what appears to be the mudguard. This Panzer has a full array of triple smoke launchers on the turret. Attached on the side of the Tiger is the track changing cables.

Infantry follow a battalion of Tiger.I's during operations in Poland in August 1944. During this period, to reflect the needs of a changing war situation, the *Panzerwaffe* added new camouflage colours to their Tigers that were intended to be used in place of the older shades. A new olive green was introduced, along with a new red brown.

A knocked out Pz.Kpfw.Tiger Ausf.B in early 1945. This massive Panzer was introduced in early 1944. It had a powerful 8.8cm KwK 43 gun with the length of the barrel itself over 20 ft in length, whilst the rounds weighed in at some 20kgs. This monster served on both the Western and Eastern Fronts and with its potent firepower and thick armour, it proved more than an opponent for any tank the Allied forces could field.

A battered Tiger.I destroyed by Soviet forces in Poland in the summer of 1944. Note the 8.8cm gun barrel, which has been blown off. By this period of the war desperation had filled the ranks as the Tiger dwindled in numbers. As with other Panzer units the once vaunted Tiger continued to fight on until there equipment was destroyed or they simply run out of fuel.

A well camouflaged *Jagdtiger* on a road in Germany in 1945. This was the most powerful armoured fighting vehicle in World War Two. The tank hunter was armed with a very powerful 8.8cm PaK 43 gun and was lethal against Allied armoured forces. The vehicle has more than likely run out of fuel as a fuel canister has evidently been abandoned by a desperate crew at the front of the *Jagdtiger*.

Another abandoned *Jagdtiger* this time found in a village in Western Germany in March 1945. Only 150 of these *Jagdtigers* were completed, but only 77 were ever delivered to one *Panzerjäger* battalion and one independent heavy tank battalion that fought on the Western Front. Although very effective against Allied forces the *Jagdtiger* was very heavy at 70-tons, fuel-thirsty, unmanoeuvrable, slow and very difficult to conceal from enemy targets.

# Chapter Eight

# Panzerkampfwagen.V Panther

It was soon clear by 1940 that the Pz.Kpfw.I and Pz.Kpfw.II were not suitable for combat against strong Allied tanks. When Germany attacked Russia the following year the need for a heavier fighting vehicle for the *Wehrmacht* was even more apparent than ever before. Hitler decided not to waste time and ordered MAN and Daimler-Benz to produce a prototype. The result was the design of a tank called the *Panzerkampfwagen*.V Panther or Pz.Kpfw.V.Panther.

By the end of 1942 a pre production series of 20 tanks were produced under the name *Null-Serie*. They were designated as Pz.Kpfw.V Panther Ausf.A. The vehicle had sloped armour at 50 degrees, a powerful 650bhp Maybach HL 210 engine, interleaved wheels with torsion bar suspension, and a hydraulically powered turret with a potent long-barrelled 7.5cm KwK L/70 gun.

The internal layout of the vehicle conformed to the usual pattern of German tanks. The five-man crew also followed that standard pattern. The driver and gunner/wireless operator sat in the front compartment and the main gunner, loader, and commander were positioned inside the turret.

In December 1942, a newly moderated version of the Panther was designed; it was designated as the Ausf.D. During December the Ausf.D entered production, and a month later the first variant received improved armoured protection with a re-versioned gun. The first 250 Panther Ausf.D's then rolled off the assembly line and within weeks were being transported from the testing ground to waiting railroad flatcars, where they were prepared to be delivered by rail to the Eastern Front for late June 1943. Because of the urgency of the Panther, the tank had not been fully tested on the training grounds. Even when the Panther's were hurriedly transported east the vehicles were still suffering from many teething problems inherent in all new equipment. But Hitler was determined to have the new Panther's deployed for action at Kursk. In fact, Hitler's obsession of using the new Panther for the battle had actually delayed the attack and gave the Red Army added time to transform Kursk into an impregnable fortress of mines, anti-tank obstacles, and defensive belts of anti-tank guns.

Altogether there were some 250 Panther Ausf.D's that participated in the battle of Kursk. It made a rather inauspicious operational debut on 5 July 1943. Even from the beginning of the offensive the Panther got off to a bad start, losing a staggering 125 of them on the first day alone. Many of then had difficulties reaching the front line, with a number of them suffering from engine fires caused by insufficient levels of engine cooling and ventilation. There was also widespread damage to gears, transmission, and suspension. The dense minefields too inflicted a heavy toll on the Panther. By the following day of the battle, just one-fifth of the Panther's committed remained operational.

By the end of what became the largest tank battle in military history, the Panther had failed to turn the battle. The combat experience at Kursk had been problematic for the Panther. However, despite the setback numerous changes were made in the design of the Panther and a late production Ausf.D was produced soon afterwards. The tank featured various modifications, including new suspension, gearbox and hull letterbox mount for an MG34 machine gun. In August 1943, the new improved Panther Ausf.D was scraped together, and 96 of them fought in the battle of Kharkov. During the battle the Panther finally showed how its mix of firepower, armour and mobility outclassed and dominated the battlefield. Altogether some 420 Soviet tanks were destroyed. Four months later the Panther again managed to outclass its opponents in the defence at Narva. In the early months of 1944 it repeatedly went onto to prove itself again and again. The tanks gun had tremendous hitting power, whilst its sloping front armour gave it defensive strength in any head-on encounter.

The success of the new improved Ausf.D prompted improvement of the Ausf.A. Between August 1943 and June 1944, 1,768 Panther Ausf.A's were built. During this period the Panther dominated the battlefield and soon great demands were put on the tank to fill the frontlines on both the Eastern and Western Fronts.

In spite of its success further modifications of the Panther still continued. The Ausf.G became the most numerous model with only 3,740 being produced between March 1944 and April 1945. The hull was redesigned with sloped instead of vertical armour on the lower-hull sides. It was also given additional armoured protection that was thickened to 5cm.

In short, after a difficult start to its career at Kursk, the Panther had improved significantly into probably the best Panzer that saw action in World War Two. It had culminated in its final production version, the Ausf.G, which fought in the hedgerows of Normandy in the summer of 1944, to prove yet again how a difficult opponent it was to destroy. Allied commanders reckoned that four Sherman's working together were needed to knock out just one Panther successfully. Altogether over 5,500 Panthers had been built, but Hitler's favourite Panzer was not enough to turn the tide. Allied air superiority significantly helped reduced the number of them in the field.

In order to help change the fortunes of the *Panzerwaffe* designers had produced a prototype heavy Panther tank destroyer in late 1943. Based on the new chassis of the Panther Ausf.G, the first production *Jagdpanther*. The vehicle rolled off the assembly lines in February 1944. It weighed 46.5 tons, and featured moderately heavy armour. However, the level of protection afforded by this armoured plating was enhanced by the vehicles deeply sloping angles. These well-sloped surfaces contributed to its low silhouette, which increased its battlefield survivability. The *Jagdpanther* was armed with an 8.8cm PaK 43/3 L/71 gun and carried a ball-mounted MG34 machine gun.

The *Jagdpanther* was the *Panzerwaffe's* most effective tank destroyer of the war. During its period of service 382 of them were deployed for action during the last year of the war. On the battlefield it had lethal firepower, good all-round protection, and excellent mobility. It could put most rival vehicles in the shade, but never fielded sufficient numbers to avert the inevitable defeat that was looming.

In demands for a new Panzer to challenge the Soviet T-34 tank, German designers produced the first prototype Pz.Kpfw.V, known as the Panther. In this photograph a turretless Panther is being put through a series of factory trials in order to see if the vehicle is watertight.

Standing in a water tank factory specialists check to see whether water has leaked into the Panther's engine compartment. This test was for amphibious wading and to see if the engine compartment seals leaked. The engine was housed in the rear of the hull and was flanked on each side by cooling radiators and extractor fans. Although the powerful Maybach engine fared under various tests, it was extremely complicated.

At the factory the hull underbelly of a Panther is being inspected. The chassis of the Panzer mounted eight sets of interleaved road wheels or bogies on either side. The road wheels were carried on twin torsion bars lying transversely across the vehicle.

A Panther Ausf.D still with transportation blocks attached moves across a field undergoing a series of factory trials. The first and second Ausf.D's were delivered on 24 January 1943 to the test ground at Gratenwöhr. Because the production of the Panther was hurried it had resulted in severe automotive transmission and suspension problems.

A Panther Ausf.D making its debut at Kursk in July 1943. The Panzer was rushed into the battle before it was fully ready for combat. However, in spite of the teething problems the *Panzerwaffe* deployed two Panther-equipped tank battalions for the Kursk offensive and these fought on the southern front in a separate 'Battle Group *Kempf*'.

During the battle of Kursk a Panther Ausf.D uses its powerful 7.5cm L/70 gun against a suspected Russian position. In all, some 250 Panther Ausf.D variants participated in the Kursk operation, most of which were in the 51. and 52. Panzer Battalions. In spite of Hitler's confidence in the Panther, the vehicle actually made an inauspicious operational debut and was plagued by mechanical problems.

The crew of a Panther Ausf.D pose for the camera prior to a training operation in early June 1943. This photograph was taken one month prior to the Kursk operation. Hitler had insisted that the Panther be ready for the largest tank battle in military history and even delayed the attack so it would give the manufacturers sufficient time to sort out the mechanical teething difficulties.

A Panther Ausf.D being put through its paces in order to get the vehicle ready for the Kursk operation. In spite of the mechanical problems the Panther had a very impressive main armament that was a superb anti-tank gun and extremely accurate. During controlled tests, it could hit a target 2m high by 2.5m wide, using the Pzgr 39/42 round 100 percent of the time out to 1500m. However, these levels of accuracy did not reflect the actual probability of hitting under battlefield conditions, but gunners would soon prove to be very accurate.

Another Panther going through a series of trails on the proving grounds of Gratenwöhr in early 1943. The vehicle still retains the factory Panther number '163' painted in large white numbers on the side of the turret. The tank is practising wading through water, which soon proved its undoing at Kursk when water leaked into the engine compartment.

A Panther Ausf.D rests in a field. The vehicle has received an application of winter whitewash camouflage paint that has also been applied over the interleaved road wheels. This variant mounts six smoke candle dischargers, three on each side of the turret. These were discontinued in June 1943. However, some Panthers still carried them for a number of months until they were finally removed.

The crew of a Panther Ausf.D rest with their tank during a training exercise, prior to the Kursk operation. The vehicle appears to have retained the factory base colour and the number '138' is painted in white on the side of the turret. There were a total of 250 Ausf.D's that were produced during this period, this one being the 138th vehicle.

A crew member poses with his Panther Ausf.D. The photograph shows a nice view of the 7.5cm KwK 42 L/70 rifled cannon with canvas sheeting protecting the muzzle break. The muzzle break was fitted to shorten the recoil. With the amount of smoke and gas that the barrel produced after firing, a barrel fumes evacuator was introduced in April 1943 to prevent powder gasses entering the fighting compartment.

A well-camouflaged Panther Ausf.G passes a stationary Panther Ausf.D during operations on the Western Front in July 1944. The Ausf.G variant has been fitted with an MG34 machine gun attached to the turret roof in order to protect it from both ground and aerial attack. The Ausf.G variant became the most numerous model to see action with 3,740 of them being produced between March 1944 and April 1945.

Two Panthers move across a cobbled road in Germany in September 1943. Both the vehicles have the new coating of Zimmerit anti-magnetic mine past applied over the entire tank. It is visible from the leading Panther through a letterbox shaped hatch in the glacis plate the radio-operators MG34 machine.

A photograph showing two Panthers on a training exercise in the early spring of 1944. By the time this model had been produced it had rectified most of the deficiencies and also featured a new type glacis plate with a ball mounted machine-gun, improved crew vision devices and thicker side armour.

. Panther being
nspected during one
f its trials in 1944.
he Panther had
become so readily
vailable during this
eriod; it actually
omprised of half the
trength of the Panzer
ivisions and was
ctive on all fronts,
ncluding the Western
nd Eastern Fronts
nd in Italy.

More Panthers going through a number of trials prior to their dispatch to the Eastern Front. Although the Panthers made a disastrous combat debut at Kursk, the vehicle matured and became the best all-round Panzer of the war and was available in large enough numbers to make a difference on the battlefield.

A Panther Ausf.G during operations on the Eastern Front in 1944. The improved Ausf.G had an improved crew vision devices and thicker side armour. Some of them had all-steel road wheels and a number had an early infrared sighting device, technology that was well ahead of its time.

The same Panther Ausf.G (as No.18) during operations on the Eastern Front during the summer of 1944. The vehicle has spare track links attached to the rear offside and the tanks gun-cleaning tube is attached next to it. This view illustrates how the *schürzen* were hung. Every plate overlapped each other in order to reduce the likelihood of them being easily torn off in action.

Three Panthers on a training exercise. The crews dressed in greatcoats and black Panzer field caps confer onboard their stationary machines. The leading Panther has the factory number '116' painted in white on the side of the turret.

ⵧlish troops examine a ⵧocked out Pz.Kpfw.V ⵧsf.A Panther from 2. ⵧmpanie, 1.Abteilung, ⵧnzer-Regiment 4, in Italy, ⵧring the summer of ⵧ44. This particular ⵧnther proves the ⵧlnerability of the local ⵧrrain and has become ⵧⵧck in earth and ⵧandoned by its crew.

The interleaved road wheels of the same abandoned Panther Ausf.A. The Panther wheels were spaced widely on the alternate axle, allowing the edge of the closely spaced wheel to sit slightly between them. However, this interleaved overlapping wheel system could sometimes get packed with mud and consequently freeze in artic temperatures jamming the wheels.

Another view of the same Panther Ausf.A Italy in 1944. This particular Panther that belonged to Panzer-Regiment 4 was amon[...] one of a number of units that had rushed to the Anzio sector in direct response to the Allied landings in January 1944.

A Panther Ausf.G rolls through a destroyed town in the summer of 1944. The tactical number of this vehicle is '322' and belongs to a Panzer regiments 1.*Abteilung*, 3 *Kompanie*, second vehicle of the second platoon. It carries standard stowage items on the near side and still retains some of its *schürzen* plates.

A Panther Ausf.G takes cover inside some undergrowth prior to launching an attack against Russian forces. This variant encompassed a major design of the hull which introduced sloped rather than vertical armour plates on the lower hull sides, and more steeply sloped armour elsewhere.

A knocked out Panther in Russia. The vehicles main armament has been made immobilized by an enemy shell entering the side of the 7.5cm barrel. Panther losses could have been much worse had the Russians fielded more potent anti-tank gun than their 76.2mm Field Gun Model 1942.

A very well camouflaged Panther Ausf.G in Northern France during the summer of 1944. The Panther formed the mainstay of the *Wehrmacht* efforts to resist the Normandy invasion. However, the Panzer was constantly harassed by aerial attack and was compelled finally to advance during the hours of darkness to reduce the huge losses inflicted on them.

A captured Panther Ausf.A sits abandoned by the side of a German factory in 1945. It has *Zimmerit* coating and wears what appears to be the manufacturers identification, 'FFI'. It is finished in a factory based sand colour and appears to be prepared and ready for frontline action.

A rear view of a Panther Ausf.A. The turret is at a six o'clock position. Road wheels and an idler wheel have disappeared and the circular access plate on the hull rear has been removed. Note the unusual cut down condition of the right-hand storage locker, as well as the jerry can racks inboard of each other.

Panthers lay dormant after being knocked out of action, probably in Italy in late 1944. The main Panther in the picture is an Ausf.A, readily identified by the MG34 machine gun mount and the open drivers visor on the upper glacis plate.

A group of children on board the engine desk of a Panther Ausf. A. The vehicle has a formidable coat of *Zimmerit* and wears the tactical number '412' on the turret side. Most of the suspension track of this vehicle has disappeared, as have probably all the tools and equipment, or anything else the fleeing crew could use.

An abandoned *Jagdpanther* found in German field by Soviet forces in April 1945. The *Jagdpanther* was one of the most effective tank destroyers built during World War Two. The vehicle was built on the chassis of a Panther and had a sloped frontal superstructure housing an 8.8cm PaK 43/4 cannon. The Jagdpanther entered service in June 1944 with the 559 and 654 *Panzerjäger* battalions. However, like the Panther this huge tank destroyer was numerically inadequate to deal with the growing Allied and Soviet armour and were eventually knocked out or run out of fuel supplies.

# Chapter Nine

# The Sturmgeschütz.III

From the very beginning of the war the use of mobile operations was a very important factor to the success of Blitzkrieg, and artillery played a decisive role in that new concept. However, it was soon realized that during the Polish campaign artillery units that operated as close to the battle zone with mechanised infantry, the more vulnerable the gunners were to enemy fire. What was needed was a mobile artillery piece that could keep pace with the infantry, give them a measure of protection, and provide support on the battlefield at a moments notice.

In 1936 a prototype assault gun had already been developed, but had not entered service in time for the war against Poland. The new vehicle had been fitted with a heavy short-barrelled 7.5cm KwK L/24 gun mounted on the chassis of a Pz.Kpfw.III Ausf.A. Although it was a heavier weapon that could normally be carried on the Pz.Kpfw.III, the extra space for the gun was achieved by removing the turret and attaching the gun on a fixed mount. The vehicle was designed primarily to support and fight alongside the infantry and keep pace with the lightening advances of Blitzkrieg.

In 1939 the new assault gun, now designated as the *Sturmgeschütz* or StuG.III.Ausf.A rolled off the production line. It was not until the Spring of 1940 that a series of production models went through a number of gruelling trials with five army batteries, one of them actually participating in the battle for France in 1940. Late that same year another StuG variant entered service, the Ausf.B, and the following year in 1941, a total of 548 further assault guns – the Ausf.C, Ausf.D and Ausf.E variants were delivered.

On 1 June 1941, there consisted five new independent assault gun batteries, all of which were prepared for the invasion of Russia that month. During *Barbarossa* the StuG.III were detailed to the infantry divisions that fought at focal points in the battles. In those first triumphant weeks of the invasion of the Soviet Union, the assault guns performed well in an infantry support roll. But as the war progressed, by the winter of 1941 the Soviet Army began introducing heavier armour. Consequently, the StuG.III was continually hard pressed on the battlefield and constantly called upon for offensive and defensive fire support, where it was gradually compelled to operate increasingly in an anti-tank roll. As a result, by the end of 1941 some 377 StuG.III's were lost in battle. The need for more StuG's were now greater than ever before.

By the following year a new more powerful assault gun entered service. It was designated as the Ausf.F and was armed with a long barrelled 7.5cm 40 L/43 gun. With this new assault gun it was now possible to fight the Soviet T-34.

On 1 April 1942, there were some 623 StuG.III's available on the Eastern Front, and that number rose to 1,422 by 30 June 1943. There were 788 produced in 1942 alone, 93 of which were the short barrelled variants. In May 1942, production of the final version of the 7.5cm StuG.III 40, now with the 7.5cm StuK L/48 long barrel had begun. This final variant, the Ausf.G, came off the production line in 1943 and rushed straight into service. It was armed with an MG34 machine gun for local defence and featured periscopes to give the commander some protection as he surveyed the local terrain.

By 1943, the StuG.III had become an extremely common assault gun, especially on the Eastern Front. Its low profile and mechanical reliability saw their employment grow on the battlefield. Some 3,041 of them were made operational in 1943 alone. A further 4,973 StuG.III's entered service between 1944 and 1945. In total some 8,587 were produced with over 800 earlier versions.

From 1943 until the end of the war the assault guns were slowly absorbed into the Panzer units, Panzer and Panzer grenadier divisions of the *Wehrmacht* and *Waffen-SS*. However, in spite of the assault guns numerous advantages, equipping

A StuG.III in action on the Eastern Front in 1941. This self propelled gun was armed with a short-barrelled 7.5cm KwK L/24 gun, which was already being installed in the Pz.Kpfw.IV. As illustrated in this photograph the StuG.III proved a valuable support vehicle.

A StuG.III halted on a road during operations in Russia during the initial phase of operation Barbarossa. The requirement for the production of a low silhouette tank necessitated mounting the gun in a fixed superstructure, which was installed directly on to the chassis of a Pz.Kpfw.III.

some of the Panzer units did not blend well with the nature of the Panzer. Yet, because of the lack of tanks in the dwindling ranks of the Panzer divisions, the StuG.III was used alongside the Panzer until the war ended. Throughout this period the StuG provided its worth as an invaluable anti-tank weapon. In a number of last-ditch battles it continued to show its true capabilities as a tank killer. But, despite its proven tank-killing potential and its service on the battlefield, the StuG.III gradually deprived the infantry of the vital fire support for which the assault gun was originally built, in order to supplement the massive losses of Hitler's Panzers.

A StuG.III. Ausf.B at a workshop. This assault gun has the early narrow 38cm tracks as well as the narrow road-wheels. The engine deck of the vehicle has been covered with tarpaulin sheeting, probably to protect mechanical work being undertaken to the vehicle engine compartment.

A StuG.III. Ausf.B moves along a road amid various assortments of vehicles including horse drawn transport and infan[try] on bicycles. The Stu[G] has a national flag draped over the tu[rret] for aerial recogniti[on] This common procedure by crew[s] especially during th[e] early phase of the campaign.

In the harsh Russian artic conditions two StuG.III assault guns move through a snow-covered village. In Russia these assault guns soon proved how valuable they were especially in an anti-tank capability. They were designed primarily as a close support weapon for infantry, but in 1941 lacked a machine gun for local defence.

A StuG.III being loaded with ammunition. The assault gun carried a variety of high explosive including smoke and armour piercing rounds. However, the short 7.5cm gun was only capable of penetrating 40mm of 30-degree armour at 1000m.

A StuG.III Ausf.B advancing along a muddy road. Ausf.B weighed 21.3 tons and was powered by a 300 bhp Maybach HL 120 TRM V12-cylinder petrol engine. It had a maximum road speed of 45 kph with a operational range of some 161 km.

A StuG.III crosses a pontoon bridge during its onward journey in Russia in 1941. In Russia it was initially planned that the Panzer divisions were not going to be worn out in attacks on defending enemy units. Instead, the assault guns with supporting infantry were supposed have been given this role.

Advancing towards the front lines in the summer of 1941, infantry hitch a lift on board a StuG.III. These assault guns not only provided ample anti-tank capability but also supported and rescued infantry on the battlefield. However, the success of the StuG.III soon saw the Red Army using similar combat vehicles in large numbers.

A StuG.III pulls on to a road in the summer of 1941. The vehicle has spare track links attached to the rear along with two spare road wheels fitted on the engine deck. During the first year of the Russian campaign the assault gun proved indispensable to infantrymen and the elite *Waffen-SS* formations alike.

A StuG.III has become imbedded in thick snow and the crew of a Pz.Kpfw.III are attempting to pull the assault gun out by using tow cables. Although tracked vehicles were capable of coping with snow and mud, the Russian winter of 1941 had been so severe that it actually ground to halt the bulk of the German armoured striking force.

An infantry support vehicle probably belonging to an unidentified *Gebirgsjäger* unit has developed a mechanical problem and broken down on a road in southern Russia in 1941. A soldier appears to be attempting to re-start the vehicle by cranking the engine shaft with a crank lever. In the background a stationary StuG.III rests by the side of a muddy road with one of the crewmembers standing next to it.

A photograph vividly illustrates the various components that went into making a striking force in Russia during the summer operations of Army Group Centre in 1941. Here a number of StuG.III. Ausf.B's lead the armoured drive following by a multitude of support vehicles and motorcycle combinations.

The new StuG.III Ausf.G. With the increase of Soviet armour on the Eastern Front the StuG.III was frequently called upon for offensive and defensive fire support. In light of this in September 1941, Hitler ordered that the StuG.III be up-armoured and re-armed with a long barrelled 7.5cm gun to give it genuine anti-tank capability.

A *Sturmartillerie* crewmember flexes his muscles in front of his fellow comrades in 1942. They are standing next to their StuG.III, which appears to be laden with various supplies on the engine deck. All the crew are wearing the field-grey *Sturmartillerie* uniform that was issued to StuG crews from 1942 onwards.

A company of StuG.III Ausf.G`s being loaded onto a train for transportation to the Eastern Front in 1943. All the assault guns have the longer barrelled 7.5cm StuK 40 L/48 cannon, which both necessitated modification of the frontal superstructure and increased the vehicles over all weight to 21.3 tons.

A StuG.III. Ausf.G with a coating of winter white wash paint rests on a forest road in 1943. The Ausf.G variant was the first assault gun to carry a 7.92mm MG34 machine gun for local defence and it was better protected, mainly through the addition of 30mm thick appliqué plates bolted on the front.

A company detachment of StuG.III. Ausf.G's move through an Italian square in 1943. The production of the StuG standardised on the Ausf.G model and during 1943 alone German factories produced 3,041 of them, and a further 4,973 during 1944-45.

Three StuG.III. Ausf.F's advance through a Russian field. These assault guns are identified primarily by the figuration of the hull's rear plate. This variant was produced in late spring 1942 and mounted a long barrelled 7.5cm StuK 40 L/43 cannon.

A Luftwaffe crew of a StuG Ausf.G on the Eastern Fron in 1943. During the war the Luftwaffe had many field divisions including Flak units however by 1942, number ground staffs, flak units and recruit depots were transferred to become Arm infantry. A number of Luftwaffe units also receive Panzers and assault guns to The Hermann Göring Panz Regiment was the most recognized as the premiere tank unit of the Luftwaffe.

Three StuG.III. Ausf.G's negotiate a typical muddy road in Russia in 1944 following a heavy downpour of rain. The leading vehicle has intact *schürzen* and a visible coating of anti-magnetic mine paste. The *schürzen* has an unusual camouflage scheme of a heavily over-sprayed mottle pattern of olive green, with red and brown over the dark sand base.

A StuG.III has halted in a cornfield in the summer of 1944. It is evident by the appearance of other vehicles in the field that this StuG is being covered with straw in an attempt to help conceal it from enemy aerial observation. By this period of the war losses of tracked vehicles through aerial attack mounted to some forty percent of the entire armoured force. In northern France this figure was much higher.

A StuG crew pose for the camera with their parked assault gun inside a forest clearing in the summer of 1944. The crewmen wear the field-grey version of the Panzer crewman's uniform, which was a distinction of the assault gun troops, who were officially still part of the artillery branch.

A line of StuG. IV's stop on a road. The vehicles are finished in a thick coating of Zimmerit paste. Note the rain gutter system just forward of the commander's cupola. Fitted to the side of the vehicle it has spare road-wheels and track storage, as well as mounting rails for *schürzen*.

A knocked out StuG.III. Ausf.G. somewhere in northern Italy in 1944. The vehicle has most of it suspension blown away with the track being thrown forward. The roof plate too is missing, making the StuG very difficult to be salvaged from the battleground.

A column of StuG. IV's passing a line of spectators. By 1944 it had become more obvious that the assault gun could no longer satisfy all the requirements as a vehicle or a weapon. The 7.5cm 40 L/48 cannon had been introduced more than two years before and both the Allies and Soviet forces were applying newer technology to compete against the StuG.

A line of later variant StuG.III. Ausf.G's stationary on a road in northern Italy in 1944. By this period of the war there had been a dramatic rise in the production of this model allowing them to be employed in both the *Wehrmacht* and *Waffen-SS* assault gun batteries.

A stationary StuG.III. Ausf.G on the edge of a town that has seen some intensive fighting. The vehicle has intact *schürzen* and the troop emblem assault gun badge painted on the side next to the national cross marking. Canvas sheeting has been draped over the roof of the vehicle in an attempt by the crew to help conceal it from aerial attack. The crew can be seen at the rear of the vehicle.

# Chapter Ten

# Tank Destroyers and Self-Propelled Guns

From the very beginning of the war, tank destroyers and self propelled guns were created in direct response to the urgent demand for guns able to counter heavier enemy armour and support the Panzer divisions lack of artillery. They eventually both became a valuable contribution on the Eastern Front against heavy Soviet armour, and provided vital support for the troops in battle.

The first real tracked tank destroyers were converted Pz.Kpfw.I Ausf.B's. They were armed with a Czech PaK 4.7cm anti-tank gun, which was mounted on the chassis of a Pz.Kpfw.I Ausf.B. The mounting for this weapon was protected on three sides by armoured plating and provided a limited traverse of 15 degrees. The vehicle was designated as a *Panzerjäger* Sfl auf Pz.Kpfw.I.Ausf.B and saw service in France, Balkans and on the Eastern Front. This early type tank destroyer remained in service until 1942.

Another early tank destroyer to make its debut in France was the *Schweres Infanteriegeschütz 33 Bison* or sIG 33. The vehicle was armed with a powerful 15cm gun that was mounted on the small chassis of a Pz.Kpfw.I Ausf.B. This heavy tank destroyer had a crew of four and formed the heavy infantry gun platoon of SS grenadier and Panzer grenadier regiments from 1940 until the end of the war.

The sIG 33 was no match against heavy armour. Although it had a potent anti-tank gun, its poor blend of the overly high superstructure and weak chassis meant that it was far from adequate to meet the growing demands of a highly mobile and versatile tank destroyer.

On the Eastern Front the ever-increasing opposition including heavier and more powerful modern Soviet armour, finally compelled the *Wehrmacht* to call upon more mobile and powerful anti-tank weapons. In direct response a number of improvised tank hunting machines were developed which carried lethal anti-tank weapons on the chassis's of converted Panzer variants. The development of the *Marder*.III *Panzerjäger* was the first of a long series of improvised tank destroyers. The *Marder*.III was armed with a captured Russian 7.62cm M36 field gun mounted on the chassis of a Pz.Kpfw.38 (t). The tank destroyer had lightly armoured three sided shield fitted directly onto the chassis. But with no real protection from the elements, apart from the engine, the crew spent most of the winters, cold and miserable. In spite of this, the vehicle proved a valuable asset and provided the *Wehrmacht* and *Waffen-SS* with mobile artillery support on the front lines. With the success of the *Marder*.III came the development of a similar vehicle that was armed with a powerful 7.5cm Pak 40/3 L/46 anti-tank gun. It utilised the Pz.Kpfw.38 (t) Ausf.H chassis and quickly earned respect on the battlefield against the T-34 tank. Between 1942 and 1943 some 418 of them were produced. In 1944, another modified version made an appearance on the Pz.Kpfw.38 (t) chassis, the *Marder*.III Ausf.M. In total 975 were built to meet the never-ending defensive actions in the East.

In 1942, another tank destroyer was developed, the *Marder*.II. It was armed with a 7.62cm gun. Later versions carried the 7.5cm Pak 40/2 anti-tank gun. Both guns were constructed on the Pz.Kpfw.II Ausf.D and Ausf.E chassis. Although vulnerable to enemy fire, it proved a valuable tank destroyer against the growing Soviet armour.

With the success of the *Marder*.III and *Marder*.II came the development of the *Marder*.I. This vehicle was armed with a 7.5cm gun, converted from captured models of the French, fully tracked Lorraine carrier. In total 185 of these vehicles saw action. Though only lightly armoured, they proved very potent machines, primarily being used by some of the most elite units in the Wehrmacht on the Western Front in 1944.

In the last year of the war, the *Marder*'s were slowly phased out to replace them with the *Jagdpanzer*.38 (t) Hetzer. This became the most advance tank destroyer on World War Two. With its distinctive silhouetted armoured superstructure it carried a deadly 7.5cm Pak 39 L/48 gun on a specially widened Pz.Kpfw.38 (t) chassis. By the summer of 1944, it began joining the anti-tank battalions until the very end of the war.

Another rare tank destroyer to see action in the later part of the war was the improvised version of the StuG.III assault gun – the *Jagdpanzer*.VI tank destroyer. The final version of the machine was designated as the Pz.Kpfw.IV/70. It was armed with a 7.5cm StuK 42 L/70 gun and proved more than capable of dealing with Soviet armour.

One of the most deadly tank destroyers that was a good all-round weapon of the war was the *Panzerjäger*.IV Nashorn. This potent vehicle was armed with an 8.8cm duel anti-tank/anti-aircraft gun. It was built on the chassis of a Pz.Kpfw.IV and had a four-man crew. Some 494 of these vehicles were built in 1943 and were used extensively on the Eastern Front in a 'fire-brigade' role in order to stem the inevitable withdrawal from Russia.

In spite of the might of enemy armour and the use of various adapted tank destroyers deployed to deal with the increasing threat, the Germans were also aware of the great lack of self-propelled artillery. Whilst the new tanks destroyers were entering service on the Eastern Front, the development of a new batch of self-propelled guns was produced. In 1942, the *Wespe* and *Hummel* were to be the answer for providing mobile artillery support to the infantry.

The *Wespe* was armed with a 10.5cm light field howitzer in an open boxed like structure attached to the chassis of a Pz.Kpfw.II. Between 1942 and 1944 some 683 *Wespe's* left the factory for operational duties and played a significant role in a number of major offensive and defensive actions.

Another self-propelled gun that was almost as popular as the *Wespe* was the *Hummel*, and was very similar in design to the Nashorn. This was a very effective weapon that mounted a standard 15cm heavy field howitzer adapted on the chassis of a Pz.Kpfw.III/IV. A total of 666 *Hummel's* were built until the programme was finally terminated in 1944.

One of the most powerful self-propelled vehicles to see action was the *Sturmpanzer*.IV or *Brummbar*. The tanks main armament was a short-barrelled 15cm StuH 43 L/12 gun and was built on the chassis of a Pz.Kpfw.IV. It was developed primarily to support infantry and was first see in action at Kursk in July 1943. Although the Brummbar was heavy and slow, this did not hinder its intended role of providing artillery support.

Both the Russian and their Western Allies had become increasingly concerned by

Panzergrenadiers support an attacking sIG 33 heavy infantry gun during the Western Campaign in 1940. This rare machine formed the heavy infantry gun platoon of Panzergrenadier regiments from 1940 until the end of the war. This box like structure was built on the chassis of a Pz.Kpfw.I and was armed with a 15cm heavy infantry gun.

During a pause in the fighting at Kursk in July 1943. One crewmember appears to be reading a map whilst sitting perched on the front offside mudguard of a *Marder.III*. This vehicle was the first of a series of improvised light tank destroyers, and was built on the chassis of a Pz.Kpfw.38 (t). This particular vehicle is fitted with a captured 7.62cm Russian Model 36 anti-tank gun.

the devastating impact of these tank destroyers and self-propelled guns. Despite their relatively small numbers, the rest of the war saw these various models score sizable successes on both fronts. But with severe shortages of fuel and spare parts and the badly depleted Panzer divisions in which they served, they continued fighting a bitter defensive action until they run out of fuel, broke-down or fell into enemy hands.

A *Marder*.II in action on the Eastern Front in 1943. The *Marder*.II tank destroyer had a high box-like structure with steeply sloping sides built on the chassis of a Pz.Kpfw.II. It was armed with a 7.62cm gun mounted on top of this superstructure within a three-sided gun shield.

The crew pose with their camouflaged *Marder*.III on the Eastern Front in 1943. The *Marder*.III mounted a new German 7.5cm Pak 40/3 L/46 anti-tank gun. Its redesigned superstructure with longer shield that afforded better protection for the crew was married to the chassis of a Pz.Kpfw.38 (t).

A *Marder*.III receives some serious attention from a maintenance team during summer operations on the Eastern Front in 1943. The 7.5cm anti-tank gun barrel is being installed by the use of a specially adapted hoist. These independent maintenance teams kept the vehicles in fighting condition and owed much to the success on them on the battlefield.

Two crewmembers pose for the camera with their *Wespe* howitzer gun on board a flat bed railway car. This vehicle was armed with a 10.5cm leFH 18/2 L/28 gun and protected by a lightly armoured superstructure mounted on a chassis of a Pz.Kpfw.II. The vehicle served in armoured artillery battalions but were lightly armoured, and as result many of them were lost in battle.

A *Wespe* being transported across a river in 1943. The large 10.5cm gun limited ammunition stowage to only 32 10.5cm rounds. Consequently ammunition had to be carried in a gun-less *Wespe* ammunitions carrier that stowed an additional 90 rounds of ammunition.

A Nashorn *Panzerjäger* IV has halted next to the battlefield whilst the crew confer with another Nashorn crew in 1944. This tank destroyer is armed with an 8.8cm PaK 43 duel anti-tank/anti-aircraft gun and was probably one of the best all round weapons of the war.

Allied soldiers examine a captured Nashorn in Germany in March 1945. Branches from trees have been applied to the side of this vehicle in order to help camouflage it from enemy observation. The high profile of the Nashorn made it hard to conceal, but its long-range gun enabled it to fight further distances than other tank destroyer.

A stationary *Hummel* in early 1945. The *Hummel* mounted a standard 15cm heavy field howitzer in a lightly armoured fighting compartment built on the chassis of a Pz.Kpfw.III/IV. This heavy self-propelled gun carried just 18 15cm rounds, but was a potent weapon against Soviet armour.

A *Hummel* undergoing maintenance at a workshop in Poland in the summer of 1944. A crewmember can be seen in the driver's compartment. The vehicle was mounted in a large four-sided superstructure toward the back of a lengthened Pz.Kpfw.IV hull. The engine was moved forward from its normal position at the rear to a more central location to provide more room at the rear as a fighting compartment.

On board a flat bed railway car is a Hummel destined for the front lines of Russia in the spring of 1944. Five of the six-man crew pose for the camera with the vehicles 15cm gun. The first *Hummel's* to see action was at the Kursk offensive in 1943. Thereafter each Panzer division was supposed to have at least one *Hummel* battery.

A *Hummel* on the move in early spring of 1945. This vehicle is carrying various provisions under the 15cm gun on the frontal deck, including rolled up canvas sheeting used to help protect the crew against the weather. On the move the crew travelled in the fighting compartment with only the radio operator and driver seated under all-round cover.

A knocked out Jagdpanzer 38 (t) Hetzer tank destroyer photographed by Soviet forces in April 1945. The Hetzer was a very effective tank destroyer and was designed on the chassis of a Pz.Kpfw.38 (t). It was armed with a 7.5cm PaK 39 cannon, and for secondary armament it had one roof-mounted 7.92mm MG34 or MG42 machine-gun.

Soviet soldiers examine the same knocked out Hetzer tank destroyer. It was not until July 1944 that the first tank hunting battalions began to be equipped with the Hetzer. These vehicles were primarily used to pick at formations of much larger Allied tanks before retreating. Its potent 7.5cm gun was effective against the armour of most of its opponents.

Soviet soldiers march passed a destroyed *Jagdpanzer* IV/70 during operations in Eastern Germany in March 1945. The *Jagdpanzer* IV/70 was a well-liked and effective tank destroyer, which had knocked out many Russian tanks. The big 70-calibre version of the Panther's 7.5cm Pak 42 gun was installed on Hitler's personal orders. But by late 1944 combat was defensive and their attributes on the battlefield mattered little.

A pre-production *Jagdpanzer.IV*, designated as the *Jagdpanzer.IV A-O*. The *Jagdpanzer.IV* featured a superstructure with sloping surfaces and periscopes for crew vision atop of a Pz.Kpfw.IV chassis. The tank destroyer was armed with a 7.5cm PaK 39 with a barrel 48 calibres long and this was supported by two front-mounted machine guns.

A *Sturmpanzer.*IV *Brummbär* assault gun has probably run out of fuel inside an Italian town in late 1944. The *Sturmpanzer.*IV was a variation on the standard Pz.Kpfw.IV for providing mobile artillery support to the infantry. The high-box like superstructure housed the 15cm StuH 43 assault howitzer. The vehicle is heavily coated with Zimmerit mine paste and has intact *schürzen*. Camouflage netting, canvas sheeting and foliage can be seen on the vehicle.

A *Sturmpanzer.IV Brummbär* assault has been knocked out of action against Allied forces in Germany in the spring of 1945. The vehicle appears to have been cannibalised by the crew before there hasty retreat. After its debut on the Eastern Front three tank battalions were equipped with the *Brummbär* and they fought on the Western Front and in Italy. They're intended role was providing heavy fire against fixed positions at the forefront of an infantry assault.